THE LORD'S PRAYER

THE LORD'S PRAYER

David Pawson

Anchor Recordings

First published in Great Britain in 2015 by
Anchor Recordings Ltd
72 The Street, Kennington, Ashford TN24 9HS

**For more of David Pawson's teaching,
including DVDs and CDs, go to
www.davidpawson.com
For further information,
email info@davidpawsonministry.com**

ISBN 978-1-909886-71-1

Printed by Lightning Source

Contents

This book is based on a series of talks. Originating as it does from the spoken word, its style will be found by many readers to be somewhat different from my usual written style. It is hoped that this will not detract from the substance of the biblical teaching found here.

As always, I ask the reader to compare everything I say or write with what is written in the Bible and, if at any point a conflict is found, always to rely upon the clear teaching of scripture.

David Pawson

Matthew 6:9–15 *(NIV)*

'This, then, is how you should pray:

"'Our Father in heaven,
hallowed be your name,
your kingdom come,
your will be done,
on earth as it is in heaven.
Give us today our daily bread.
And forgive us our debts,
as we also have forgiven our debtors.
And lead us not into temptation,
but deliver us from the evil one."

For if you forgive other people when they sin against you, your heavenly Father will also forgive you. But if you do not forgive others their sins, your Father will not forgive your sins.'

SEE ALSO LUKE 11:2–4

OUR FATHER IN HEAVEN

When people say that if everybody lived up to the Sermon on the Mount that would be all that we would need, I am inclined to agree with them. The trouble is I haven't yet met anybody who could do so. Those who say that kind of thing usually don't know the Sermon on the Mount and don't realise how much it says about prayer, fasting and all kinds of other things.

"And when you pray, you must not be like the hypocrites for they love to stand and pray in the synagogues and at the street corners that they may be seen by men." I often wondered whether anybody would ever do that, at least in Britain. But when in Arabia I found that there was a Muslim, a man of some position, who used to deliberately go to the main crossroads in the centre of the town just at the hour of prayer, so that he was caught in the most public place at midday. People called him, in Arabic, "the man who prayed at street corners".

Jesus was born in the kind of world where people paraded their piety. It is possible for us to do it in other ways. Jesus said, "Truly I say to you, they have their reward." They will be rewarded for it, but their reward will simply be what men say about them. "But when you pray, go into your room, shut the door, and pray to your Father who is in the secret place. And your Father, who sees in secret, will reward you. And in praying, do not heap up empty phrases as the Gentiles do, for they think that they will be heard for their many words. Do not be like them for your Father knows what you need before you ask him." That is the context. Jesus then taught us how to pray.

Most people pray. Many people say their prayers. Prayer is universal in all religions and all races. There is nothing specifically Christian about people praying. It is surprising how many people in this country think they are Christians because they say prayers.

The real thing that makes prayer Christian prayer is not so much *whether* you pray as *what* you pray. It is not so much the fact that you might close your eyes and say something to a being you call "God", it is what you say that matters. Indeed, it has been said that you can tell more about someone's theology and character by studying their prayers than anything else. Of course, most of us don't get an opportunity to do this. If we are honest, I think most Christians would say that it is in the realm of prayer that they need to learn, more than in any other realm. It is here that we all feel we are in the primary department. It is here that we find it most difficult perhaps to be a true Christian. Therefore, it is very easy for this side of the Christian life to slip.

Our Lord both practised prayer himself and told others to do it. Therefore that makes it a must. You cannot be a Christian unless you pray. In the Sermon on the Mount he said: *when* you fast, *when* you give alms, and *when* you pray. He didn't say "if", he assumed that we would do it as a normal part of the Christian life.

Early one morning the disciples, lying asleep on their mats in a little room in the fishing village of Capernaum, stirred at dawn and began to sit up and look around. They noticed that the bed where Jesus had gone to sleep the night before was empty. They thought they had lost him and they dashed into the street and looked up and down for him. He wasn't there. They went out to the hills to try to find him. Above the town they came across a little hollow and there Jesus was praying. They listened. No-one had ever talked to God as Jesus did. When he had finished, they came up to him and said, "Lord, teach us to pray." They didn't say, "Teach us *how* to pray." They said, "Teach us to pray." How could Jesus talk to God like that? They wanted some hints, some instruction that would help them to talk to their heavenly Father as he did.

It was out of this request that what we call the "Lord's Prayer" was born. We call it that, but you realise that it was not a prayer he used himself, and indeed it was a prayer that he could not have used. There are things that we have to say in prayer that Jesus never had to say: "Forgive us our trespasses." Jesus never had to say that. We only call it "The Lord's Prayer" because he gave it to us.

Before we look at it in detail, I want to look at two simple principles of prayer which he taught just before this in the Sermon on the Mount. The first is the most obvious thing and yet we are slow to learn it. *It is the quality of prayer rather than its quantity that matters.* It is a pagan idea that if you heap up prayer you are likely to get more out. The more you put into the slot machine, the more answers will come out at the other end. It is like a pagan priest in Tibet spinning his prayer wheels believing that every time the wheel goes around another prayer has gone to heaven. Or somebody with beads and a rosary might repeat the "Our Father", hoping that a number of recitations will all pile up. But none of these things gets the ear of God. The Greek word used for "much speaking" or "many words" in Matthew 6:7 is *polulogia*. Jesus is teaching about prayer and this teaches us not to think that more and more talking is going to help.

I love the story of Sir Wilfred Grenfell's conversion. Walking home from the training hospital in London where he was going to be a doctor, one night he saw a big tent. Inside there was an evangelist from America preaching. Grenfell went in, and when he sat down it was just at the point in the service where a prayer was announced and some local brother was invited to pray. The man praying got up and went on and on, prayed for all the world, every continent, every country and every conceivable situation. Oh, he knew how to pray! Wilfred Grenfell got up to leave and he might have been lost to Christ through that long prayer, but the evangelist stood up and said, "Brethren, we'll sing a hymn while our brother finishes his prayer." This so captivated Grenfell that he turned around in the tent door and said, "A man as sensible as that I want to hear." He sat down, and at the end of the meeting he became a Christian.

Do not think that you will be heard for much speaking. That will not get God's attention. He doesn't need to be told a thing again and again. We need to ask, but he doesn't need to be told. Jesus said that he knows what you need before you ask. That raises the very simple question: why ask if God knows what I need and he loves me? Let me give you the classic illustration which answers that question. There was a famous violinist who had a daughter. She learned the violin too, but from another teacher who was a second-rate musician. The father was asked, "Why is it that you are not teaching your daughter? Why is she going to a much poorer musician?" He replied, "There is nothing I would like more than to teach my daughter the violin, but I must wait until she asks me. There are things I cannot impart to her till she is ready for them and comes to ask."

Now that is the true relationship of father and child. God knows you need something, but there are things he does not do for you until you are ready to receive them, and you will be ready when you come and ask. Never get the idea that prayer is not asking. The whole of the Lord's Prayer is asking. Almost every phrase is asking. There is a kind of pious mysticism which says that the higher reaches of prayer get beyond asking for things. Don't you believe it. Jesus told us to ask, and his lovely prayer in John 17 is full of requests, and so we are to come and ask for things – not because God does not know, but because to come and ask and to seek and to knock means that we are ready.

Prayer is not valued for its quantity, but its quality. It is not how long it is, but how deep it is. We must not have formality in prayer, but we do need form in prayer. This is a lesson that it takes us a long time to learn. It has been said that without fervour, form becomes formality, but without form, fervour becomes fever. We do need fervour in prayer. We need depth of feeling in prayer; of course we do, but feeling by itself is not enough to make a good prayer.

I remember being in a prayer meeting in Belfast some years ago. The minister and I sat in that prayer meeting, and as we came out he whispered to me. It was just before a service where I was preaching. He said, "Well, if noise is power, we're in for a good time tonight!" I knew what he meant. We had plenty of fervour in that meeting, a lot of noise, but it lacked something. It takes more than noise to make power.

Jesus, when he answered the request to "teach us to pray", didn't say you should get all worked up. He gave a form or pattern of prayer. The pattern needs to be filled with meaning and fervour, but it is strange that people cannot see that we need both fervour and a form. A pattern of prayer filled with feeling is the ideal combination. In the Old Testament, they had patterns of prayer. They used the Psalms and other prayers. In the New Testament also, the Christians continued in the apostles' doctrine and fellowship and breaking of bread, and *the prayers*. They had their prayer books. I have no objections whatever to a prayer book and I hope you haven't either. But a prayer book without fervour is about the deadest thing you can get. Fervour without some kind of pattern to help it along is just generated heat that is not specific and directed, so Jesus gave a form. Now I am not sure he meant us to use it like parrots, though it is helpful to use it together and in the same version because then we can all pray together. But he said, "When you pray, pray like this." In other words, this is the kind of prayer you should pray. Therefore, in your private prayers, may I suggest that you take the Lord's Prayer and see if your prayer follows this pattern. The Lord's Prayer was given to us to use in private, in your room.

Now let me make six little points about this prayer. First of all, I want to underline once again that it is such a *brief* prayer. You can get through it by speaking it in about thirty seconds. Yet, it is one of the biggest prayers I know. It is a prayer that you could use in a little gap in the day when you have nothing to do. It is interesting that some Jewish scholars have said that there is not a phrase in this prayer that you can't find in the teaching of Jewish rabbis. That may be true, but I have read a Jewish version of the Lord's Prayer and it is three times as long. If there is one new thing that Jesus brought to this prayer, it was to give it brevity.

Secondly, it is *simple* – straightforward and easily remembered. It is not a prayer only for the highly educated but a prayer for everyone. The youngest can pray it; the dying can pray it.

Thirdly, it is a *profound* prayer. You may think about this prayer all your life and still not understand it fully. I wonder how many really understand what it means to say, "Lead us not into temptation". Do you understand that phrase? You can think about this prayer all your life and still it is fresh.

Fourthly, it is a *comprehensive* prayer in that it covers everything. You study these six petitions, and every one of them in principle covers a whole field of need.

Fifthly, it is a *universal* prayer. You can take it anywhere in the world. You don't need to alter it, it has been translated into hundreds of languages. It is so universal that anybody can pray it.

Finally, it is the most *challenging* prayer you will ever pray. I would say of the Lord's Prayer that it is not so much a prayer, more a way of life. If you really pray this and mean it, your life will be altogether different afterwards. It will produce a reverent, active, submissive, dependent, forgiving, careful Christian. That is a list of six things that are produced in your character.

Now let us look at the first phrase: "Our Father in heaven". Every prayer needs a name and an address and here it is: "Our Father" – there is the name; "in heaven" – there is the address. First of all, look at the person to whom we pray: "Father". That is why it is called the "family prayer". Therefore it is a prayer which only children may use. I can't call the Duke of Edinburgh "Dad". There are a few people who can; I don't know if they do. I expect that they do, or something even more familiar. But I can't go up to him and call him "Dad" because he is not my dad. There was one person who was my dad, and I and my sisters had the right to call him that. Unless you are a child of God you have no right to use this prayer. Not everybody is a child of God. A poet said: "The world is an orphanage, full of people without a father." That is a wonderful description. Until you know Jesus Christ as Saviour you are an orphan; you are in a universe without a Father. But when you have come to know God as Father, then the universe becomes a very different place. It is a cold universe until you know God as your Father, and then it becomes a home. Even the next life simply becomes the Father's house – home.

I think of the story of the little girl sitting in a railway carriage all by herself and a person saying to her, "Aren't you afraid to be travelling alone?" She replied, "Of course not, my daddy's driving this train." This is the feeling that we have as children of a heavenly Father. "Aren't you afraid of this great big universe? Aren't you afraid of nuclear war? Aren't you afraid of men? Aren't you afraid of history? Aren't you afraid of death?" No, of course not, my Father is directing this universe.

The word that Matthew and Luke record here for "Father" (the Greek is *pater*) is a family word, and the phrase that follows immediately "in the heavens" reminds you that your heavenly Father is not exactly like an earthly dad; in some ways he is, but in other ways he is not. He is holier than any dad you ever knew on earth. It means that he is more powerful than any dad on earth. It means that he is more hurt when you do wrong than any dad you knew on earth.

I had a wonderful earthly father who, when I was a boy, punished me and I'm glad he did. I remember those painful occasions well because there were few. But when they were there, they were dreadful. I thank God for an earthly father who chastised me because he loved me and because he wanted me to grow up to be a Christian gentleman. In the same way if I say "Father in heaven" I have a father who will do that, a father who is not a grandfather, not a sentimental old man who just spoils children, but a father who takes very seriously my character and my life – the heavenly Father.

The other little word in this initial phrase which I want to underline is "our". Now bear in mind that this prayer was given for private use. I have been misunderstood for saying this and I hope you will not misunderstand me now: there is no such thing as private prayer. You can never pray by yourself. Therefore, when you get into the bedroom and shut the door and you are all alone, say, "*Our*..." and "...give *us*". This is one of the best correctives in private prayer that I know, to stop you ever praying in a selfish way. If you pray for things that you can ask for others, you will stop being selfish in your prayer. So if your need is health, then you are also praying for others who need health. If your need is for peace and freedom from worry then you are also praying for others who are worrying. See what that does to your prayer. You will then not be able to pray without thinking of other people. "*Our* Father, give *us* today *our* daily bread" – even when you are alone, use the personal pronoun plural and then you will not forget your brethren. You are praying as a member of a family, and you don't forget the rest of the family.

Now finally (and all this is simply by way of introduction), let me show you the amazing pattern that there is in this prayer. There are six petitions and they divide into two lots of three. One to three are concerned with God's needs and four to six are concerned with ours. Do you notice the order? Pray for what God wants before you pray for what you need and your prayer is healthy. Pray for what you need first and your prayer is unhealthy. Father, *your* name, *your* kingdom, *your* will; then *our* bread, *our* sin, *our* deliverance. That is the order of prayer. Examine your private prayer. Do you begin by praying for what God wants? That is how Jesus taught us to pray, and that again puts a lovely perspective on prayer.

There is even a deeper significance in the sets of three. In each case the first is something we need from the Father, the second from the Son, the third from the Holy Spirit. Take the second three: who provides our daily bread? The heavenly Father. Who obtains forgiveness for our sins? Jesus, who died on the cross. Who will keep us out of evil? The Holy Spirit, dwelling within us. Do you see the pattern?

The same pattern is there in the first half. The three things you pray for first are the three things God wants from mankind: reverence, allegiance, and obedience. *Reverence* so that they only use his name properly. *Allegiance* as citizens of his kingdom, acknowledging that he is King as well as

19

Father, and *obedience* to do his will on earth as the angels do it in heaven.

The three things we pray for others and ourselves are these: *dependence*, a sense that everything that we eat and wear and do comes from God; *forbearance*, that we might be forgiving to others as well as receiving forgiveness from him; *deliverance* from evil, which you need every day of your life. Take those second three another way and you see the pattern unfolding. The first of the second group is concerned with your present: daily bread. The second is concerned with your past: forgive us our debts (or trespasses), as we have already done. The third is concerned with tomorrow, your future: deliver us from evil. Do you see the pattern? All of life is contained – your present, your past, your future. This prayer is bringing the whole of life to Father, Son and Holy Spirit. What could be more wonderful, and it is all in about fifty words!

HALLOWED BE YOUR NAME

When I was a little boy, my father took me to hear one of the greatest preachers of those days. I cannot remember what he said except for the word "God", which he kept using. I have never heard a preacher before or since who could say "God" as he did. It has stuck in my mind from boyhood. Just think of that, a preacher who could just say "God", and you were in the presence of the Almighty.

We have seen how the Lord's Prayer is a pattern prayer. Now what does this phrase "hallowed be your name" mean? Have you ever noticed that the Ten Commandments and the Lord's Prayer follow much the same pattern? The first half of the Ten Commandments is concerned with God, the second half with people. Furthermore, the first, second, and third commandments correspond to the first, second, and third phrases in the Lord's Prayer. Commandment number one is "You shalt have no other gods before me." Prayer phrase number one is: "Our Father". Commandment number two: "You shalt not make any graven image, anything that is in the earth, any beast or any likeness". Why? Because God is heavenly – Our Father *in heaven.* You don't know what heaven is like so you can't create an image. Third commandment: "You shall not take the name of the Lord your God in vain. Third phrase in the Lord's prayer: "Hallowed be your name. Do you see the parallel? Pray as you live and live as you pray – that is the message.

As we look at the meaning of "Hallowed be your name", two main headings will help us: *revelation* and *reverence.*

You cannot *reverence* the name of God until you have received the *revelation* as to what the name means.

Before I went to a new church as pastor, unsurprisingly hardly any of the members would have known the name "David Pawson", so it would not have meant very much to them at all. Once I had become their pastor it meant at least that they knew who I was. You might say that they had had a "revelation". The point I am trying to illustrate is that a name does not mean anything until you have had a revelation as to the person behind it. A name is just a name, and every name or combination of names should be unique to that person. I think it awfully unfair to saddle someone with a name that is going to tie them to someone else's nature. I knew a boy called "David Livingstone". You can guess when he was born, or at least when his parents were born, and who their great hero was. He is now a missionary in Africa. The poor chap had no other choice I think, but God called him! He married a congregational minister so they became the Reverend and the Reverend David Livingstone, which I think just about seals it. But the poor man was given a name that tied him to someone else's nature and I am afraid there was this pressure on him all the time. My own father was called Cecil, after Cecil Rhodes, and he kept having this presented to him as a boy.

Rev. Poplar, that great Methodist missionary in the east end of London, was once christening a baby and said, "Name this child."

The parents said, "Call him 'Genius'."

He said, "Pardon?"

They repeated it: "Call him 'Genius'."

He said, "But do you mean genius – somebody brilliant?" They said, "Yes."

He said, "But you mustn't saddle this boy with this name."

They said, "Go on, call him 'Genius', we want to give

him something to live up to." That poor chap had to go to school and to every teacher who said "What's your name?" he would have to say "Genius."

One difficulty, of course, in naming children is that you don't know what they are going to be like before you name them. You can call them "Joy" but it doesn't mean they are going to be happy. You can call them "Angela", but it doesn't mean you have got a little angel. You can call them all the names you like. Now God *can* call a person a name because he knows what their nature is going to be like. The names God gave in the scripture always fitted people perfectly. Above all, the name Jesus perfectly fitted the baby boy born at Bethlehem, but here we have the name "God", and that name is filled with the meaning of a personality so different that this name ought to be kept very sacred. I must admit that since it really began in a big way in the entertainment programmes on television since the 1960s, over half a century ago now, I became increasingly unhappy about the way God's name has been used. The expression "Oh, my God" has become widely used as an exclamation in the broadcast media and in the ordinary conversation of unbelievers. We are praying that God will stop that kind of thing. We are praying that when people use that little word "God" they will think of who they are talking about, and that they will tremble when they use it like that preacher I heard as a boy, who just had to say: "God".

What is God's name? We don't know. I wish I could tell you. The nearest I can come to is "Yahweh". At least one modern English translation has used that to render his name. It has four Hebrew characters which we write as JHVH. Some people knock at your door and tell you it ought to be "Jehovah". They are quite wrong because "J" is pronounced like a "Y" and "V" is pronounced like a "W", so you can't get "Jehovah" out of that lot.

23

You could get "Yahweh". More important, you can get the meaning because we know what it meant even if we don't know how to say it. It means: "I am what I am." He has a name that is different because he has a nature that is different . You can't say God is *like* anyone. He is who he is. Therefore he has a name that you would never give to anybody. I have never heard anyone called "I am", have you? When you use his name, you must think of who he is.

People have different views as to who God is. Some people think of a kind of Santa Claus, an old man in heaven with a beard. Some people think of an insurance agent – that if you pay your premium you should get your benefits. To some people he is like a policeman.

But God is who he is, and "I Am" is his name. When Moses said "Who shall I say called?", he said, "I Am called you and sent you."

How do you find out who God is? The answer is that you will never find out unless you listen to what he says and watch what he does. Every psychiatrist will tell you that the first task is to *listen* to someone. You will never get to know them unless you listen to them. If you are ever going to know someone as a person and find out what their nature really is, it is your ears you will have to use as well as your eyes. Listening to what they say and seeking to realise what they are saying to you, then you know what the name stands for. That is how you get to know what God is like.

If I am going to hallow his name, three things are necessary: a belief in his existence, a knowledge of his character and a sense of his presence. I have never met anybody who hallowed the name of God without those three things.

If you don't believe that God really does exist, if you don't have a knowledge of his character – that he is holy, and pure and clean – and if you don't have a sense of his presence, if any one of these three is missing, you do not hallow his name.

It is obvious that a person who doesn't believe in the existence of God will not hallow his name. It is strange that atheists will even use the name of God as an expletive, just a word – like the man who said, "I'm an atheist, thank God." He was just using the phrase as any non-believer uses it. But you must have a knowledge of his character. If you are going to regard his name as hallowed, then you must see that he is a holy person, for hallowed means "holy". You don't treat a name as holy if the person isn't holy.

I think of a dear saint of God, a lady, very close to the Lord Jesus, and therefore very like him. When anybody mentioned her they always spoke quietly with awe and a kind of catch in their voice. Why? They hallowed her name because they had found out she was a hallowed person. This discovery of her character made them speak of her with that tone in their voice which really was quite awesome.

The third thing is that if I am going to hallow his name I must remember that I can never speak outside his presence. I am going to make a confession. I once knew a man with a most unusual surname. I remember sitting at a table once with a lot of people around. We got to discussing surnames and when we got to discussing unusual ones I mentioned the name. I said, "I've got one that will cap the lot," and I just hope there's nobody here tonight with this name. As I came out with it I became aware of a lowering of the temperature and a distinct chill in the atmosphere. The poor man was two seats away from me at the same table, and it was quite obvious he had heard. I would never have said that had I known he was anywhere near. Neither would people say, "My God" but would hallow his name if they had a sense of his presence. You can't talk about God in his absence – it would not be possible. You might talk about other people in their absence, and maybe that is why we sometimes say what we do about others in our weak moments, things that we wouldn't say if they were there. But when you have a sense that God is always there, you don't talk like this.

So if we have a belief in his existence, a knowledge of his character and a sense of his presence, we will never blaspheme that name; we will hallow it.

Let us consider seven ways in which people blaspheme that name. Number one: perjury. When you appear as a witness in court you are handed a New Testament and stand there and say, "I swear by Almighty God to tell the truth, the whole truth and nothing but the truth." Most of us who have sat in courts have listened to counsel demonstrating so clearly that someone who said that is not telling the truth. Why do they use the Bible in a court? The answer is this: the basic problem in human relationships is to get someone else to tell the truth. In a society where God was believed in, which was true in earlier days in England, it was thought that if a man swears by God to tell the truth, knowing that God is listening to every word, then surely he would tell the truth. The days have come when it is almost a blasphemy to use the Bible in court today. Not because there are so many not telling the truth, but because there are so many who take the Bible in their hands and who don't believe that God is there listening. It has become a mere formality, which is just gone through at the invitation of the clerk to the court.

I was present once when a minister of the gospel preferred to take a solemn affirmation rather than swear by the Bible because he felt the Bible had been made so cheap that way. You have the choice. It may well be that if you found yourself in that position you would rather just make a straight promise. Jesus said, "Don't swear by God in heaven or by the earth, it is his footstool. Let your 'yes' be yes and your 'no' no."

You might also commit perjury in a wedding service. "In the name of Father, Son, and Holy Spirit, I pronounce you to be husband and wife. What God has joined together let no man put asunder." Thousands of weddings a year, many of which took place in church, are broken officially – that is perjury, taking the name of God in vain.

The second thing is *profanity*. I mean what I have already referred to, just using the word "God" as an expletive, a swear word. Now every swear word that I know is destructive. What is wrong with swearing? Is there anything wrong with such words? Let me tell you what I believe is wrong with them. They all take something sacred and beautiful and smash it. There are only two deeply sacred relationships to mankind: one's relationship to God and the relationship between a man and a woman. Almost every swear word I hear comes from one of those two relationships.

I had the dubious privilege of working in a cowshed at four every morning with a man who had the reputation of being able to swear longer than anyone else in the entire district without repeating himself. Every day I had to listen to this and it struck me that every word he used took something holy and smashed it. Therefore he made those words useless for their true meaning. The word "damn" is a terrible word. It is a Bible word and it stands for that act of God which finally puts a man beyond reach of all help. If you use it flippantly, as a profanity, then it doesn't mean that any more.

The word "hell" has lost its meaning for many people because they just tell people to go there. It is a terrible thing to tell someone to go there. It is one of the worst things you could ever say to someone. I don't need to enlarge on the others except perhaps to inform you that the word "bloody" has two wrong connotations. Again it is a biblical word, but it is either destroying a sense of the blood of Christ, that is one possible origin, or it is a shortened form of "by our lady" and is a reference to the Virgin Mary.

I have noticed that when someone really meets Jesus he stops swearing, his mouth is clean because he has met someone who didn't swear and he has met someone who treats the relationship between men and God and men and women as sacred, hallowed things.

Now the third thing and it comes out of this is *flippancy*, a sense of humour that goes too far. I thank God for a sense of humour. There have been occasions when if I had not been able to laugh I would have cried, and a sense of humour can be a saving grace. I notice that saints usually have a good sense of humour but flippancy can just step over the line. Jokes about the furniture of heaven or the temperature of hell easily slip over the line, as do jokes about angels. And never laugh at the devil, never treat him as a joke, he is too subtle for that. It is wrong to make jokes about these things because again you destroy a sense of proportion. The things that are laughed about are no longer taken seriously.

The fourth way is *incredulity*. By that I mean refusing to believe in God's works and words. Someone who does not believe in miracles is profaning the name of God. One of his many names is "El Shaddai; God almighty." That name is known widely because of its having been used in a profane or flippant way. That is a name of God – he is Almighty – and a person who says "I can't believe in miracles" is not hallowing the name of God because the name of God is Almighty. Not to believe his word is to profane his name.

Fifthly: *hypocrisy*. John Bunyan wrote this in his autobiography: "I fell in with the customs of the time to wit, to go to church twice a Sunday, and there would I sing and pray with the foremost, yet retaining my evil life." Martin Luther wrote a catechism for children and he wrote this down, "How is God's name hallowed among us? Answer: when both our life and doctrine are truly Christian."

Hypocrisy does not hallow the name of God. We come to church, we take the name of Christ on our lips and then we live just like everybody else. That doesn't hallow his name because we bear his name and they will judge his name by us and say: "Well, if that is Christianity I don't want it."

Familiarity is the next thing I want to mention. We hear a growing number of phrases which are used in an over-familiar way about God. Here are some I came across: "the man upstairs"; "the old one"; "you know who"; "him up there". You can't better the Bible for phrases to describe God, and it is very easy to invent other phrases which become over-familiar.

John and Charles Wesley argued over a hymn that Charles wrote: "O for a Thousand Tongues to Sing my Dear Redeemer's Name." John Wesley wouldn't have it in his hymnbook. John won and he changed it to, "O for a Thousand Tongues to Sing my Great Redeemer's Name." "Dear" is not a word the Bible encourages us to use.

To some people the word "you" instead of "thee" and "thou" in prayer has seemed to be over-familiar and not hallowed enough. I realise that this was true for an older generation. "Thee" was considered a more reverent form than "you", but language is changing. I think it is a great pity that the New English Bible was just not bold enough to make the change. It is not necessarily irreverent to say "You" to God. It is the tone of voice in which it is said and what is said that will make the reverence clear. The Bible does not encourage two forms of speech—one to your friends and one to your Father. It encourages the same language to both.

Finally there is just straight *blasphemy*, when God's name is used to support evil things. Jesus said to his own disciples: "There will come a day when people will kill you in the name of God." In the name of God terrible things have been done. In the name of God, men have gone to war and killed. In the name of God, men have had inquisitions and they have tortured those who would not believe in Jesus. This is blasphemy. It is tragic when the name of God is used for something that God could never approve.

We remember the cross. Why was Jesus put to death? He was put to death on one charge: blasphemy. Behind all the political charges was one: he calls himself "God". Now which was right in the prayer that Jesus prayed the night before he died? He said, "I have hallowed your name. I have given them your name. I have brought them into your name. I have done all this in your name." He had also taken the name of God, "I Am", and had applied it to himself, and said, "I am the bread of life. I am the shepherd, the good shepherd." "I am the way, the truth, and the life." "Before Abraham was, I am." They cried, "Blasphemy. They decided that he must die.

Of course, according to their law, not to hallow the name of God was worthy of death. So when they put him on trial they said, "Are you the son of the living God?" He said, "I am." The high priest tore his clothes and said, "You've heard it out of his own mouth. Blasphemy, he deserves to die, to take the name of God like that." Do you know that the Jews hallowed the name of God so much they didn't dare to say it? Do you know what they called God in the days of Jesus? The called him "the name". They said, "Well you pray to the name," or, "The name bless you." They didn't dare to use it. Here was Jesus saying, "I Am," and so they put him to death and they did it in the name of God. In the name of God they condemned the Son of God to die.

But the name of God and the nature of God was (and is) in Jesus. If you want to know what the name means, then look at Jesus. He gave us the name of God because, for the first time, we know what that name really means. We can see what it stands for. He gave us the name of God, and they took that name and they stripped that name and they spat on that name. They whipped that name and they nailed that name to a cross. That was the blasphemy. Jesus died because he was supposed to be one who did not hallow God's name. It was the scribes, the Pharisees, Pilate and Herod, the soldiers and the runaway disciples who were not hallowing the name of God that day.

God has many names, but the one I love best is "love". Jesus was hallowing the name of God. Jesus never joked about God. Jesus was never flippant or profane about God. It was men who were profane and they cursed him. Even a thief crucified next to him cursed and blasphemed, but Jesus hallowed the name of God.

What then are we praying for when we say, "Our Father in heaven, hallowed be your name..."? We are praying for two things. First, that people may come to know what his name stands for; that when they hear the word "God" they may think of the holy, heavenly, almighty being before whom they will one day stand to render their account. Second, that we and they may not only have a revelation of who God is, but may reverence who he is, and behave reverently towards our Maker.

YOUR KINGDOM COME

We are thinking about three words, yet there is so much we could say about them. One of the dangers of using a set form of words again and again is that we say them without thinking about them, and without anything going through our minds, but this is one of the most difficult phrases in the Lord's Prayer to get right and to understand. When we say "your kingdom come", what are we praying for?

One difficulty is that so many different interpretations are given. There is a further difficulty that even in the English language the word "kingdom" means three different things. Sometimes it means a place. I have a passport for the United Kingdom and I have to show it whenever I go out of this country and step over a certain geographical boundary, and I have to show it when I come back in. On my passport the word "kingdom" refers primarily to a place on a map. The word "kingdom" can also refer to a group of people: citizens, subjects, wherever they may be, whether in a particular place or not. This meaning is not found as frequently today in English. The third meaning is hardly ever used at all, and it refers to a power. Now we don't know what the word "kingdom" means because we are used to a constitutional monarchy, and the monarch in a modern society has little or no power. Mind you, that does not mean that the monarchy is not valuable. The monarchy in Britain is valuable not so much for the power it wields as for the power it keeps out of other people's hands. So, for example, the law is under the crown rather than under the government. But the Queen does

33

not rule – as a constitutional monarch she is a figurehead, and therefore we find it difficult to use the English word in its third meaning: power.

So in Britain, that is the order in which we use the term "kingdom" – a *place* most frequently, a *people* occasionally, a *power* hardly ever, but if you went to the Middle East, those three meanings are turned upside down. They hardly ever call a place a "kingdom". There is only one that I know of – Jordan. They do not often call a people a kingdom. A kingdom means the power a man exercises.

Before I went to Arabia, when I was a boy studying geography, I thought that the deserts of Arabia were divided into squares, and that if I went out there I would see a long straight fence, straight across the sand, that then turned at right angles and came back to the coast and this was one of the Arab kingdoms. I got to Arabia and went out in a Land Rover and found no fences, just moving sand dunes. Where were these nice square lines on the atlas? They don't exist. There is no way of marking the boundary. So how do you know what kingdom you are in? You know because the power of a sheikh is to be found in that area. In other words, you soon discover whose power you are living under as you move up the coast of Arabia, and part of my job was to travel right through that region. As I did so, I moved from one kingdom to the next. I never showed a passport, I never went through a barbed wire frontier, I never knew that I had got there until I found that people feared this man instead of that man; that this sheikh's power had ceased and that sheikh's power had taken over, and so I had moved into a new kingdom. This is the meaning in the Bible, because the Bible was not written in the United Kingdom, it was written in the Middle East.

The kingdom of God means the power of God, not a geographical area, not even a people. It means the power that he exercises, which is why Jesus once said, "There are some standing here listening to me who will not pass away before they see the kingdom of God come with power." In other words, you are going to get the power of God in your lifetime. They did, of course, on the day of Pentecost. If we crossed out the word "kingdom" in our Bible and put in the word "kingship" I think we would probably do a lot better. Or even if you crossed out the word "kingdom" and put in the word "power" you would find that it fitted. But we will keep the word kingdom because we use it in the Lord's Prayer.

Now comes a problem. The word "kingdom" is used hundreds of times in the Bible. We need to look at how the word changed in its meaning and developed and filled out until now when we say "your kingdom come" we almost need to know the whole Bible before we can understand what the term means. Let us start in the Old Testament. Israel was a kingdom before she had a place and before she was a people, because the power of God came upon her. The Israelites were just a bunch of nobodies, slaves with no money, no land, no government; no community, no rules, nothing that makes a nation. Then God in his almighty power got them out of that land, and defeated the Egyptians for them. Having got them under his power, he then made them a people and he gave them his laws, community rules down to the last detail of personal hygiene, which would enable them to live as a people. Then he said, "Now I'll give you a place," and he gave them the promised land of Canaan. You see the order: the power, then the people, then the place; but the kingdom began when God stepped in in power; then they became a people; then they got the place, the kingdom of Israel.

They did not need either to be a people or a place before they could understand what the phrase "kingdom of God" meant. They were meant to be a kingdom unique in the world. The only kingdom in the world without a visible king – that was what God meant them to be. God was to be their kingdom, their king, their kingship, their reign and their ruler. God would give them their laws, God would lead them in battle and he would do everything for them that any other nation's king would do. They were to be his kingdom, and he would do it.

But, alas, the people of Israel. when they looked at the other nations who all had strong men as kings, came to God and they said, "We want a king, someone on a big horse in the battle." And God said, "Alright, I will give you a king, but I warn you, in exchanging a divine king for a human one, you will soon find yourselves in trouble." They chose a fine, strong, big, handsome man called Saul and he was mad. So they sought another one, and God guided them to a man called David. He was a good man, and they never knew such peace and prosperity as under his kingship, but he too was a man, and he had feet of clay. His weakness appeared and after that happened David was never the same king again. Then they had Solomon, a man with grandiose building schemes, who was full of pride and instituted slavery in Israel. He so raised discontent that the day he died civil war broke out and they finished up with two kings: Jeroboam in the north, Rehoboam in the south.

From then on you can read all about it in the two books of Kings. The royal standards went down and down. Occasionally there were good kings like the boy Josiah who came to the throne at twelve years of age, but for the most part they were a bad lot. So they never had such a good time as under King David, and it was almost natural that when they prayed "your kingdom come" they were meaning, "Give us another king like David." That was their prayer, Still to this day, after three thousand years since David reigned, when the Orthodox Jew says "your kingdom come" he is is praying for another king like David.

But there were deeper thinkers who began to think like this: we asked for a human king, God gave us human kings and look what they were like; we need a divine king, yet we would love to have a human king. There was born within their minds a concept of a king of Israel who would be divine and human, who would be like a Son of Man and yet would be the Son of God. They gave this figure a title: "The Anointed One", which in the Hebrew language is Messiah and in the Greek language is Christ. They prayed for this king who would be the best of both worlds, divine and human.

If they had gone on praying like that, it would have been wonderful, but they didn't. More and more the political human side dominated the heavenly divine side. They were overrun by the Egyptians, the Babylonians, the Assyrians, the Syrians, the Greeks, the Romans. Time and again they tried to get their own king. They succeeded for a few years in the days of the Maccabees with Judas Maccabeus, but they lost the throne very quickly. When Jesus was born they were suffering the indescribable dignity of being reigned over by a puppet king of the Roman enemy, and a foreigner at that, a hated Edomite called Herod was ruling over their land. There was a resistance movement fighting for the kingdom and for their own king, and now when they prayed "your kingdom come" they saw a political uprising, a nationalist riot that would put a Jew back on the throne. In the middle of all that, an angel came to a young virgin of probably about fifteen years of age and said, "The Holy Spirit will come upon you. You are going to have a baby even though you have not known a man." And then I give you the exact words the angel said: "The Lord God will give to him the throne of his father David, and he will reign over the house of Jacob forever and of his kingdom there shall be no end."

That young girl was directly descended in the line of David, and through an amazing series of circumstances and a decision made a thousand miles away by a Roman emperor, the baby was born in the city of David. Through another astonishing event, which occurred a thousand miles east, a number of wise men came and said, "Where is he that is born king of the Jews?" Herod said, "There is no room for another king. I am the king. The Romans have appointed me," and he killed those innocent babies in Bethlehem to try to get rid of this king.

All through our Lord's life people tried to offer him the throne. After he had fed the five thousand, we are told they tried to make him king. The Galileans would have risen *en masse* and put him on the throne. The day came when they thought he at last was going to be the king that they had prayed for when they prayed "your kingdom come". He rode into Jerusalem at the head of a mighty crowd, and he fulfilled the prophecy of Zechariah: "Behold your king comes to you, meek and lowly and riding on an ass." They thought: this is it, the kingdom has come! They shouted, "Hosanna," which means "Save us now," and they came into Jerusalem thinking that now a Jew would be on the throne of Israel again. Yet he disappointed them.

He so disillusioned them that a few days later they said, "We have no king but Caesar." He disillusioned them because he wouldn't fight the Romans. He disillusioned them because he wouldn't answer their prayer. They had prayed "your kingdom come" for centuries and he would not answer it. When they brought Jesus before Pilate, Pilate couldn't make it out. He said, "Are you a king?" Jesus said, "My kingdom is not of this world." So Pilate went out and said, "Shall I crucify your king?"

Pilate felt he was in the presence of royal power. This man who represented Roman might felt: here is a king, I can sense his authority and power. He wrote a little notice which was stuck on the cross: "This is the king of the Jews." A dying thief spotted that and sensed that he was in the presence of a king. The thief believed that one day in the distant future Jesus would have a kingdom: "Lord, remember me when you come into your kingdom." The thief had got it wrong too, the kingdom was here and now: "Today you will be with me in paradise."

We understand now what went wrong. The trouble was that Jesus thought one thing and the people thought another when they said "your kingdom come". He wanted one kind of kingdom, they wanted another. They wanted a political uprising; Jesus wanted the kingdom of heaven. They thought it was still future, he said it is here and now; you can get into the kingdom now.

At this point I will to try to answer certain questions. If it is the kingdom of God, does it include people? If it is the kingdom of heaven, will it ever appear on earth? Is the kingdom of heaven something that is going to come in the future or something that is here and now in the present? To all these questions, I am going to answer: *both*. Let me just take you briefly through our Lord's teaching on the subject. If you take your Bible and start underlining the word "kingdom" in it you make a discovery: Jesus taught the kingdom and he preached about the kingdom more than any other word. He said that the gospel of the kingdom must be preached; repent and believe, for the kingdom of God is at hand. What did he mean?

There are two things he meant – one that happens here and now in the present, and another that will happen there and then in the future. What does this mean: here and now? His message is: If I cast out demons, the kingdom of God has come upon you. If I heal the sick, the kingdom of God has come upon you. If people who are lonely and afraid are filled with new life, the kingdom of God has come upon you. When people who are in the chains of sin are set free, the kingdom of God has come upon you. The kingdom of God is something that has broken right into human history now, and you can get into it now. Indeed he said that the most unlikely people were getting into it: publicans, prostitutes. He said that the rich don't get in very easily. That means it is hard for most of us, for by his standards we are wealthy. He said that the respectable will find it hard to get in. The Pharisees just couldn't make it. The religious would find it hard to get in, but he said that anybody who is bad enough to say they are bad, and will come, can get in. Anybody who will humble himself and become like a little child and say "I've got to learn all over again. I've got to start at the beginning" can get in. Anybody who will come and say, "I need a new life, I need to be born again" will see the kingdom.

Jesus was teaching that this kingdom is something that you can't get into with a passport, you can't get into with a lot of money; you can't get in because you are very good. You can only get in if you are bad, know you are bad, and you want to be good. He said that this kingdom is like a precious pearl, worth selling everything else to get. It is worth more than anything to you. It is like a man who found treasure in a field, didn't tell anybody but went away and sold everything he had and bought the field. It is something for which someone ought to be ready to give up anything at all because it is so valuable and you can have it here and now.

Jesus said that people were entering the kingdom. It had started and was growing. It may be small, like a grain of mustard seed compared with the human race, but when it was grown it would be the biggest tree of all.

He said that it is like leaven. It works so silently. You put a bit of leaven or yeast into a lump of dough and that yeast works silently but it is working. People say, "Where is the kingdom of God?" I say: where the leaven is in the dough. People say the church is a small organisation, a tiny group of people. I say it is a mustard seed that is growing. The kingdom of God is something that is already happening and we can be in it and live as citizens right now.

That is why throughout the New Testament, not only in the Gospels but in the letters too, people are living in the kingdom. Paul writes to the Romans: the kingdom of God is not meat and drink. It is not material things. However needful those may be, and however important it is that Christians feed those who are hungry and thirsty, it will not get them into the kingdom because the kingdom of God is not meat and drink, not something physical. The kingdom of God is righteousness and joy and peace in the Holy Spirit.

When Jesus said you will see the kingdom of God come with power in your lifetime, he meant it, and on the day of Pentecost they saw the power of God come. They were enjoying the kingdom of God. Almost every letter in the New Testament refers to living in the kingdom, preaching the kingdom, enjoying the kingdom; knowing what it is like to have the power of God in your life now. That is the kingdom, and it is interesting that an early manuscript copy of the Lord's Prayer says "let your Spirit come".

I came across a wonderful story about a Russian boy who was a Christian. He was ordered by the authorities to go and fight an evil war for Russia and he refused in the name of Christ. He was brought to trial in a court. When asked why, he said he could not do this under God. The judge said: "But my son, you are talking of the kingdom of heaven and this is not come yet." The boy replied, "Your honour, it may not have come for you, but it has come for me." That is a tremendous answer.

For many of us in church the kingdom of God has come. We are in it. We are enjoying the reign of God in our lives: God ruling our circumstances; God making all things work together for good because we love him; God in charge of next week – and that is the kingdom of God here and now.

But is that all? If so, then what we are praying for when we say "your kingdom come" is simply that more and more individuals will enter the kingdom. Is that all we are praying for? It is not all, so we need to look at another side.

If half of our Lord's teaching of the kingdom says it is a present experience, the other half of what he says is that it is a future expectation; something that is not yet. It is something that is now and something that is not yet. It is this paradox that has foxed so many interpreters who cannot seem to hold both at once, so you have people going to one or the other extreme. I believe it is both. What then is yet to come? Why did Jesus teach us to pray "your kingdom come"?

At this point I must remind you of something that you already know. There is another kingdom in this world as well as the kingdom of God. There is the kingdom of Satan. When our Lord said the kingdom of God is breaking in upon you, it is at hand, it is among you, he didn't say it is within you – that is a bad translation, he said: "It's among you" he also spoke of the kingdom of darkness, disease, death, the kingdom of Satan. This is the problem. If the kingdom of God has already come, why is it that people are dying around us, why is it that there is disease, why is there violence, why are lives being ruined, why are drug addicts dying before they reach thirty? Why is all this happening?

It is because the kingdoms of this world are not the kingdom of God, they are the kingdom of Satan. When Jesus came to the earth, the devil offered to make a bargain with him, that he would give Jesus all the kingdoms of the world. Jesus didn't say that they were not his to give. They were. The devil has world politics in his grasp, and Jesus acknowledged that. The devil is controlling the world. Jesus spoke of him as the god of this world, the prince of this world, the ruler of this world. What we are seeing in the world is a confrontation between two kingdoms which are utterly opposed to each other. Jesus spoke about rescuing individuals out of the clutches of the kingdom of Satan.

That is what we have to understand, and many of our Lord's parables of the kingdom tell us that these two kingdoms will go on side by side until the close of the age. He puts it in picture language: the wheat and the tares will grow together till the close of the age; the sheep and the goats will graze together till the close of the age; good and bad fish will be in the net; wise and foolish virgins. He is constantly saying they are both together but all these parables say that a day will come when one of the two will disappear altogether. The wheat will be gathered into the barn and the tares burnt.

Who sowed those tares? The devil, in the field of the world. There will come a day when the good and bad fish are sorted out, and the bad ones thrown away, and when the sheep and the goats will be separated. That is when the kingdom will have come universally. It has come individually, but it has not yet come universally. So the kingdom of God is something that individuals can get into now, and then they can pray "your kingdom come" for the day when the kingdom comes universally.

Now, of course, if what we saw at the beginning is right, the kingdom can only come when the King comes. That sounds a bit obvious, but there was a time when England was a commonwealth. There was no king in England, and there were those who wanted a kingdom again. How did they do it? They smuggled Charles II back into England and the kingdom was restored. You cannot have a kingdom without a king. When will the kingdom come on earth as it is in heaven? The answer is: when the King gets back. My understanding of the expression "your kingdom come" is summed up in the last prayer of the Bible: "Even so, come Lord Jesus." When the King comes, the kingdom will come.

The Bible tells me that when the King comes, he will reign over the earth. The last king on earth will be Jesus. Can you imagine what it will be like when he is king? We will have world peace for the first time. There will be no need for armies, navies or air forces, for the first time. "They will beat their swords into ploughshares and their spears into pruning hooks. Neither shall they learn war any more." When Jesus is on the throne on earth, he will demonstrate what can be done in righteousness and justice when a human King who is divine at the same time – with all that means – reigns over the affairs of mankind. He will then also take the ancient kingdom of Israel and bring them back in and restore them to the kingship of God and put them under the reign of God again.

Consider the Ascension. What did Jesus say just before he ascended? What did the disciples say? Jesus said to them, "All authority in heaven and on earth is given to me. Now you go and preach to everybody." Then he said, "But wait until you have got the power." He is virtually saying: wait until you are enjoying the kingdom in power, and then go out and preach the gospel of the kingdom to all the nations until the end comes. But then they said to him a very interesting thing. Still hidebound in their nationalist thinking, they asked him when he would restore the kingdom to Israel. He didn't say he would never give the kingdom back to Israel, but he told them that it was not for them to know.

The Bible tells us that one day even the ancient kingdom will be brought back into the kingdom of God. Israel is as godless a country as ours is – only 10% go to the synagogue every Sabbath. That nation will be brought back into the kingdom, not as an exclusive national thing, but as a centre of world religion. All the nations shall say, "Come let us go up to Jerusalem. Let's go up to the city, the mountain of the Lord. Let's go to him through them," but that is not the end of it all. The Bible also speaks of a final, triumphant moment when Jesus takes all the kingdoms of the world, for he must reign until he has them and then hands them back to the Father. The old earth goes and there is a new heaven and a new earth, and the kingdom of God covers heaven and earth.

So you pray that, universally, God's reign may cover the whole heaven and earth. The practical question is: do you really want this to happen? Unlike a constitutional monarch, the God who is King actually rules. When man tries to rule himself, he fails. Man was never made to govern himself but to be subject to a King, and when I pray "your kingdom come" I am saying: "Lord, be king of my body; be king of my mind; be king of my soul; be king of my ambitions; be king of my career. You will reign in my life; you have absolute authority in my life. I want your kingdom to be manifest in me, and I am praying that everyone will accept this authority." Do you really want that?

It is nice to think that a King is going to come, but when he comes, he comes as King, and when I invite Jesus to be my Saviour, I also invite him to be my King and to take over complete control.

YOUR WILL BE DONE

I once went to see a woman whose baby had been killed by a drunken driver as the baby sat in its pram. The woman said to me, "I suppose we must accept the will of God." She must have seen a strange expression in my face, because she then said, "Mustn't we?"

I replied, "I'm sorry, I don't believe this was the will of God. I don't think we must blame God for drunken drivers." I said, "I think I do know what the will of God in this situation is. It is what you are going to do with this experience that could be his will."

This phrase "your will be done" is one of the most abused phrases in the Lord's Prayer. Taken out of its context and used to express a kind of fatalistic attitude to life is all of a piece with such sayings as "just one of those things". I am sure that this is not the kind of meaning our Lord intended us to put into the prayer: "your will be done on earth as it is in heaven." What does it mean? Let me begin negatively by saying what I believe it does not mean. Sometimes you have to clear the decks before you go on. So what does it not mean? Some emphasise the word "your" in it and give the wrong emphasis: "*your* will be done". That may denote resentment, which is a negative attitude, or resignation, which is a neutral attitude, and neither is the attitude that our Lord meant us to express.

There are very few people who use the phrase with resentment, but one poet said that he felt that life was something like a chess game, playing against a master player who always won, and that no matter what move you made, he made a move that won the game, and therefore you were in a kind of helpless vortex of circumstance. God would just move you around and do this and that to you, and there was nothing you could do to break out of it. This is an attitude of resentment.

In some of the Lord's people there is an attitude of resignation to circumstances, as if these are the only things that could happen. Robert Louis Stevenson in *The Garden of the Soul* writes: "There is a plant called wintergreen or resignation, otherwise known as the false gratitude plant. It is a showy plant, but leaves little margin for profit. I will not have it in my garden. Root it out. Out with it, and in its place put a bush of piety, but see it be of the flowering sort." That is quite a quotation!

What is wrong with saying "whatever will be, will be" or "It's just one of those things"? I found that even RAF pilots had this kind of fatalism. They said, "If your number's up, your number's up. When you take off that day, if your number's on the plane, you've had it." That was sheer fatalism, and it was a defence mechanism against life, as if saying this to themselves said also, "It couldn't have been altered, and nothing could have been done about it. You've just got to live with it." The Greeks had a version of this called stoicism – after the stoics, who taught that everything that happens is the will of the gods and there is nothing you can do but accept it and resign yourself to the fact that you are a pawn in life's game, pushed around by powers too big for you.

Do you know what the word "Islam" means? It means "submission" and the word "Muslim" means "surrendered one". In the Middle East I found that a favourite phrase among the Arabs was "Inshallah", which means Allah wills. I remember seeing an Arab who had laid out fish in the sun to dry for his winter food, and the rain came. It only came two or three times a year in that area. I said, "Aren't you going to get your fish in? The rain will ruin it."

"Allah harim," he replied, and he just sat down. This is one of the things from which the Muslim world needs to be delivered by Christian faith – the resignation, the fatalism and the sense of submission to powers that cannot be changed. That is their religion.

That great Christian Archbishop William Temple used to say we have turned a phrase that was a battle cry into a wailing litany – and I think I understand what he meant. What is wrong with this interpretation? What is wrong with saying that "your will be done" means we just accept everything that is? Three things are wrong with it. First, it assumes that everything which happens is God's will, and it is not. There are things that happen which are not God's will.

The second reason why it is wrong is that it assumes the only person who is able to do God's will is God himself, and that is against all the teaching of the Bible. If when I say "your will be done" I put the emphasis on the word "your", it may imply that nobody else can do God's will. The prayer is not that God will do his will, but that someone else may do it.

The third reason why it is wrong is this: the word "will" must be very carefully understood. I don't want to turn you into a Greek scholar, but I want to tell you there are two words in the Greek language, both translated unfortunately by the word "will" in English. Our language isn't big enough to cope with the Greek. One of the words means "decree". The will of God is his decree, which means that when God decrees a thing, nothing can stop it. There is another word which means his wish or desire, and the trouble is that the English word "wish" is too superstitious and too soft a word to convey the strength of the desire.

There is a world of difference between saying God's

decree must be done and praying "your desire be done", and the word used here is desire and not decree. There are certain things that are God's decrees. God decreed that there should be a world and there was and nothing could stop it. God decrees that the world will end one day and that is his decree and nothing can stop it. God decreed that Jesus Christ should be born of the Virgin Mary and come and die for us, and nothing could stop that. But when you come to a statement like "he wills that all men should be saved", I notice that the word "wills" is "desires" or "wishes" and that is a different matter.

Therefore I would like to translate this I think more accurately: "Your wishes be done on earth, as they are done in heaven." In other words, this prayer is not a prayer of resignation, accepting what is inevitable; it is praying that something will happen that will not otherwise happen unless you pray. It is praying for something active, not passive; something positive, not negative; it is praying that something may be done. The emphasis should be on the fourth word: "your will be *done*". If we don't pray this, then it will not be done. It is not something to accept with resentment or even resignation, but something to *do*. That is why I told that dear lady: "It is what you do with this now that is going to demonstrate the will of God – it is doing what he desires."

So what does it mean? It means not to *accept* things, but to *choose* things; not to sit down and say, "Oh well, we must accept." It means to say: I am going to ask what God's will is in this situation and do it, by his grace. I am asking that the earth should do his will as well as heaven. The emphasis in the Lord's Prayer is on the verbs, which are all active verbs: hallowed; come. It is activity—God's activity, our activity, doing something. Anybody who prays the Lord's Prayer has got to do something about it afterwards. It is much too active a prayer to sit and just pray or sing.

In John 9 they came across a man blind from birth. The disciples, speaking to Jesus, assumed it was the will of God that the man had been born blind. Was it due to his sin or to his parents' sin? They thought it was obviously God's will and that they had to accept the situation, but how did it come about? Jesus showed them that the will of God was that something should be done about the man – and he gave him sight. His reply to their question about the will of God was: we must work the works of him that sent me. In other words, here is something to be *done*.

However true it is that there are some things in life that it is the will of God that we accept and transform and make beautiful however terrible they are, nevertheless when we pray the Lord's Prayer, that was not what Jesus was referring to. He was wanting people to pray "your will be done as it is done in heaven". Well, how is it done in heaven? Let us look at how it is done. How do the angels do his will? They do it willingly, they do it continually all the time; they do it completely and they do it quickly.

At this point the prayer becomes very personal, because to pray that prayer and not to do anything is hypocrisy, which is why one saint of God used to pray "your will be done", then add in a whisper after that: "and done by me". Your will be done and done by me on earth as it is in heaven – that involves three things. First of all, the willingness to discover God's will. I wonder if you still know anybody who writes "DV" when they write a letter. I still get a few letters from people who do this. *Deo volente*, the Latin words for "God willing." What does a person mean when they say or write this? Do they only mean they will do such and such a thing unless God stops them, or do they mean "I will do it if I have discovered that this is what he wants me to do"? That is a very different thing. Most of the times I have seen "DV" in a letter, I have discovered that it is from someone who has already made up their mind to do something, and is in a sense saying: unless he does something drastic to stop me.... If you say "DV" you ought to ask first whether you ought to do whatever it is or not.

I remember once receiving a letter inviting me to speak at a well-known convention. I was writing back to them, and I nearly put "I will come on such and such a date, DV." I thought, "What hypocrisy! I haven't asked God if I should go." So I got on my knees, and God said, "No, you must not go." Furthermore, he said something else to me. He said, "And I don't want them to have that convention either." I wrote to the leader of the convention: "I must tell you that as soon as I began to put 'DV' into this, I discovered it wasn't 'DV' at all. It was not his wish that I come, and I must also share with you that he seemed to say to me that it was not his wish that you hold this convention."

They wrote back and said, "We have cancelled the convention." I met the organisers of the convention later and they said, "You know, that really was the will of God that we did not have it that year. We now know that we must hold it next year and we are going to come back to it with much fresher minds. It had become a routine for us." Now that's what "DV" means – that you find out before you write it whether you should be doing it, and if you should be doing it why put "DV"? Because he won't stop you if you have discovered what his will is. So the first thing is to discover it.

Now may I say a loving word especially to young people? You come to points where you need to discover the will of God. There is one aspect of guidance which is sorely neglected in Christian circles. Guidance can come through praying, through the direct impressions on the soul of the Holy Spirit, and it can come through reading the Bible and through a text, which springs out of the pages and says, "Do this." It can come in other dramatic and non-dramatic ways, but the one channel of guidance that I have found well-nigh infallible is to go to other experienced Christians and lay the situation before them and say, "Will you seek guidance for me as well?"

It really is amazing how many of us, immature Christians as we are, seem to think that we have got an infallible telephone line direct to heaven and never need to consult other people. If a thing really is of God, then it will stand the test of being shared with God's saints, and it is amazing how necessary that is to us. Are you considering a job, a marriage, something else important? Go to a group of senior Christians and ask them to pray and ask them to tell you what guidance they receive.

I remember one pastoral situation I had. It was the most complicated decision I had ever had to take as a minister, and I just did not know what to do. I looked at a number of possibilities, and I went to those in the church who were much better Christians than I was and said to each, "Will you pray, and will you come and see me in a month's time and tell me what you think?" A month later they came and they told me independently the same thing, and I knew what I ought to do.

There was a young man in a Baptist church and he didn't know whether he was called to the ministry or not. Sometimes he thought about it, sometimes he didn't. Sometimes he was sure he ought to and sometimes he was full of doubts. So I said, "Look, I want you to speak to the whole church and I want you to tell them you don't know whether you ought to be a minister," and he did that, at a church meeting. For three months the whole church prayed about it and sought the Lord's will, and three months later the church unanimously said, "You are needed in the ministry," and he went. Now he was still not sure himself, but he said, "This is how Saul and Barnabas were called."

There is a duty on us when we say "your will be done" – to discover it, and to test the discovery from all angles. The devil loves you to make up your mind in a hurry without thinking about it, without telling anybody else about it, so that you can't test it, but the call of God can be tested by time and advice. When I went to a minister as a young man and said, "I feel called to the ministry," he said, "Go away and come back and tell me that in eighteen months." Was that good advice? Wouldn't it discourage people, maybe putting them off for life? Don't you believe it! If you are called of God you can't be put off for life.

I came back eighteen months later and said, "I must be in the ministry." He said, "That's what I was waiting for. You just said last time 'I feel called.' Now you say, 'I must.' Now I'll help you." He did, and he started me off. I thank God for the wisdom of that man.

So there is a duty to *discover* God's will, secondly there is a duty to *do* it. A word that has become unmentionable is duty. I don't know when I last heard that word from this generation. There is a kind of Christianity that thinks duty is a dirty word – that you shouldn't go to church out of a sense of duty. Whoever said that? The Bible says: "neglect not the assembling of yourselves together as the custom of some is." You have a duty. Some people think you should only pray when you feel like praying. But who said that? This word "duty" was on our Lord's lips. If you want to know what the Bible says about duty, read the last chapter in Ecclesiastes: "This is the whole duty of man: fear God and keep his commandments." I am not talking about saving yourself by doing good works. I'm talking about fearing God and doing your duty.

So when a Christian does a service for God in the church or anywhere, he doesn't want thanking and he shouldn't be thanked. Why? Because Jesus said that when the servant has done all his master has commanded him, he has only done his duty. As a preacher, I am only doing my duty when preaching. What is wrong with doing your duty? We have a duty to God to do his will.

A certain man had two sons, and he said to one boy, "Go and work in the vineyard," and he said, "Alright, Dad," but he didn't go. Then he said to his other son, "Go and work in the vineyard," and the boy said, "No", but he later did. "Which of the two...?" said Jesus. Downright, down-to-earth duty is perhaps 90% of the successful Christian life. Obedience is a word that comes again and again in the scripture, and you never learn to be a good Christian until you learn to do God's will.

The third thing: not only to discover it and to do it but to *delight* in it when you do even a distasteful job – do it because you're doing it for the King of kings, and to delight in his good and perfect and acceptable will. So it means *resolution*. We can see that this phrase in the Lord's Prayer is not resentment and not resignation, it is resolution and, one more thing: *renunciation*.

Now if only we could realise the difference between resignation and renunciation we would understand what this phrase means. What do I mean by renunciation? A parent once said to me, "I don't have any trouble with my child's willpower; only with my child's won't power!" I know what they meant. "Won't power" – you see, if I am to do the will of God, something has got to happen to my will first. There are very few situations in which I can do his will and mine. Sometimes God graciously allows us to do something for him that we like doing, but much of the time I cannot please him except by denying myself. In other words, there is only room for one will in any one life. It is either his or mine, and if I am going to do his, mine has got to be crucified. The capital "I" has got to be crossed out, and that is renunciation.

It is not resignation because it is freely chosen, because it is cooperation with God – but it is definitely self-crucifixion.

Renunciation is not giving in to God but giving to God. It is asking God to take your will and break your will that you may be at your best.

One of the jobs that I was engaged in when I worked on the farm was breaking in horses. When we first began, the horse would rear and fight. It was a question of a battle between your will and the horse's will, and the horse would buck and gallop. It was a struggle. Just to get a saddle on was a mighty triumph and might take a morning, but when the horse's will was broken and the horse's strength was available, then to climb on its back and go galloping over the fells on that horse, and to know that the horse was one with you, that your wills were one and that therefore you could enjoy life together and be a team—that is the difference.

Sometimes, early in our Christian life, the biggest struggle is between the Lord and "I", and he is breaking us in so that he can use us and together do his will. There is one person, of course, who exemplifies this supremely. There is one person who demonstrates perfectly the meaning of "your will be done". It is Jesus. In the Garden of Gethsemane I notice he uses the word "wish" not the word "will." He says "your wish be done". He is not being forced to the cross, he is not being decreed into it, he is being called to it, and it is God's wish that he die. He says: nevertheless, not my wish, but yours be done.

GIVE US TODAY OUR DAILY BREAD

We are studying the Lord's Prayer now as a model for our own private devotions – as the perfect prayer, if there can be such a thing. It came from the lips of Jesus, who never once talked about the "problems" of prayer because he assumed it was normal and natural for a son to talk to his father.

Most of us pray more sincerely when we feel our need. This particularly applies to the phrase "Give us today our daily bread". We can go on eating, we can go on buying food in this country, and the people who don't say their prayers seem to have just as much food as we do. Their fridges and freezers are stacked and they don't need to ask God for daily bread, so there are many who honestly feel that this phrase is a bit of a hypocritical thing to pray.

Should we then cut out this phrase for the affluent West? Let's look at it a little more deeply. Here in this one short prayer we are being given a pattern and the pattern is that the heavenly things must come before earthly things in your prayer, but the earthly things must follow the heavenly things.

We have already seen that we are to pray first for God's honour, for reverence for him, for allegiance to him, for obedience to him – before we bring any earthly need. We are to think of what God wants first. That is a rule in prayer. Maybe a lot of our prayer life is stunted, selfish and dry because we start with ourselves. We should begin with heaven, but having said that, we should come down to earth and pray about the most practical things.

I remember a dear old lady in the Shetland Islands who lived in a little croft house that had a downstairs room, and an attic loft where she slept on a mattress on the floor. There was a vertical ladder up the wall to the upper room. She was crippled with rheumatoid arthritis and the next door neighbour used to pop in occasionally at night. One night she was there when the old lady went to bed. She saw her go to the foot of the ladder and get hold of it, then stop, put her head down and close her eyes. The neighbour asked, "What on earth are you doing? Are you alright?"

She replied, "I'm just asking the Lord to help me upstairs."

"Well I'm here tonight, I'll help you upstairs. You don't need to pray tonight," the neighbour said.

"Ah, but you're not here every night, most nights you're not here," came the reply.

Then the neighbour said, "Well you don't think God's bothered about you getting up a ladder, do you?"

The old lady then said a profound thing which I have never forgotten: "If he could not help me in little things I would not trust him for the big things. If he could not help me in earthly things I couldn't trust him for heavenly things."

Now she had a profound understanding. There is no detail of our life too small, too practical to be of God's concern. If we have a real need it does not matter what that need is, we can bring it to God in prayer.

The next thing you would understand if you saw my study. There are times when I can't find something – enough said! Have you ever been like this? Many times I have got to the point where I need something very badly. I may need it to help someone. I search and I still can't find it and I close my eyes for an instant and say, "Lord, where is that thing? You know where it is, tell me where it is." Again and again I open my eyes looking at it. It is the most astonishing, simple, down to earth experience, and others have this kind of experience too. If God cannot help us in the practical, little things, what is the point of asking for big things? Have you indeed got the faith to ask him for big things if you can't ask him for little things?

"Give us today our daily bread" is an utterly practical, down to earth petition, yet we will spiritualise it. Some people have so driven a wedge between the sacred and the secular that ordinary bread seems to them much too down-to-earth a thing to pray about, so they spiritualise this phrase. The Catholics have spiritualised it in a sacramental direction. I remember when I first was given a Roman Catholic Bible, Douay version. I read through the Lord's Prayer and came to the petition: give us this day our "supersubstantial" bread. This seemed to me to stick out like a sore thumb and then I noticed there was a little asterisk and a note at the bottom, referring me to daily mass. Now that is one way that it has been too spiritualised. When our Lord said "Give us this day our daily bread" he was not referring to the communion service.

In case anybody thinks I am throwing bricks in one direction, let us through one in mine. We take this phrase "daily bread" and we put it in front of Bible study notes. Have you had your daily bread today? – referring to scripture readings, and that is not what the Lord meant either.

In one sense it is right to spiritualise it because Christ is the living bread, but I want to get us right down to earth. Neither the sacramental nor the scriptural interpretation of this phrase is what I want to give you. I want to think here about *bread*, and it may seem naïve to begin by saying that he does not say "give us this day our daily cake" or "give us this day our daily jam." We are told that most of us need about 1200 calories a day. You probably get between two and three thousand on your normal diet, and if you are a glutton you could be putting much more than that into your body

– and your body doesn't need that. This is about practical daily needs, enough to live on – not luxuries, not fancy food but just sustaining bread of life.

William Temple said that Christianity was the most materialistic of all the world religions. He meant that it says more about bodies that any other religion. Almost every other religion in the world talks about "souls" and getting souls away from bodies into nirvana or some other state in which we are finished with the body. Christianity is the only religion that emphasises the body as something God saves – not only by healing in this life but by replacing it and re-creating it in the next life. God will not finish saving you until he has saved your body. The redemption of your body is part of his plan. Why? Because these bodies, wonderful organisms as they are, were given to us to be temples.

We spend a lot of money on elaborate buildings for God but our bodies are to be his temple. They are important, to be looked after, and God knows this – he made our bodies to be the temple of the Holy Spirit. Therefore, when Jesus walked this earth he didn't only offer forgiveness, he also healed and he fed. He told people to get up and walk and he gave people food to eat. He was concerned about it. I think his divine compassion and interest in ordinary human needs is marvellous.

At the feeding of the multitude, Jesus was not watching the faces of his congregation with the thought, "Do they think I'm preaching a good sermon? Are they listening to this?" He saw that they looked hungry, they needed a good square meal before setting off on that long journey home. Isn't that thoughtful? So he gave them bread and fish.

Now let us look at the words "give us today our daily bread" in reverse order. First: "bread". The Bible states that man shall not live by bread alone, but the first meaning of that phrase is man shall live at least by bread. It means that he needs bread to live, and a corpse can't be converted, and a man who is starved to death cannot be reached for Christ.

This sounds again a simple, obvious statement, but I came across a prayer of Queen Elizabeth I. Every morning, in her private chapel, she would use a prayer she had written out for herself, and here is one of them: "They that are snared and entangled in the extreme penury of things needful for the body cannot set their minds on Thee, O Lord, as they ought to do; have pity on them therefore, O merciful Father, and relieve their misery through Thine incredible riches, that by Thy removing of their urgent necessity they may rise up unto Thee in mind." Forget the Elizabethan English, there is the heart of a queen who is concerned about the bodies, minds and spirits of her subjects, who recognised that while people were starving it was not easy for them to listen to God.

When the Bible says that man shall not live by bread alone it is not saying that bread is unimportant, it is saying that man needs more than bread because he is more than an animal. Man needs God as well as food, and he needs to feed on God, but he cannot do that unless he has enough to eat.

Next we look at the word "daily". It seems a simple word but you would be amazed to learn that the scholars could not translate that word for a very long time. Nobody knew what it meant. It only occurred twice in the Bible – in Matthew and Luke. It had never been known in any other book in the world. There was no Greek literature that used this word (*epiousios*) so they guessed, and the Catholics guessed it meant "super substantial" and others said "subsistence bread". Then, in the twentieth century, somebody digging around in the sands of Egypt unearthed a bit of parchment and in the dry sand of Egypt parchment will survive as it won't in the wet climate of Israel. He found it had some Greek writing on it, and it was around two thousand years old. It turned out to be a woman's shopping list, and at the top of it was this word, and the sentence in which it occurred made it utterly clear what it meant. It meant "for tomorrow". The lady's list was what she needed to buy for the next twenty-four hours, which means: give us today enough to live another twenty-four hours. That's all. It is such a simple little word.

Jesus said, "Don't worry about tomorrow", so it is a sin to worry. Live a day at a time. Our life is divided up by God into twenty-four hour periods. No one is really capable of living more than twenty-four hours at a time. We are to go to bed and finish that day off, confess its sins, thank God for its blessings, and go to bed trusting that he will bring us through just another day.

But of course we don't live like that. We are not living on that basis in this country and so we find it difficult, but I know that the secret of the saints is to live one day at a time. When you are really going through it, and when you are really in trouble or danger, and when you are really hungry, there is only one safe way to tackle it, and that is to say: "Lord, we'll just live a day at a time. I'm not going to worry about the day after tomorrow or next week, just give me enough for twenty-four hours."

Now the word "our". The one thing that the Lord's Prayer doesn't allow you in your private devotions is selfishness. (Incidentally, some people say we say the Lord's Prayer too often, but I would say that we don't say it often enough in private.) There may be a day when you don't feel like prayer, when you don't know what to say, when you feel dead and dry. What should you do? Then pray the Lord's Prayer that day, going through it phrase by phrase.

It will deliver you from self pity because it says "our" – "give us today *our* daily bread." Who is included? All the Lord's people. When we pray "our" we are not thinking of the whole world because the whole world are not the sons of our Father. When we say "our" we should think as widely as the whole church in the whole world – we are praying for every son of God, every child of God.

A misunderstanding that could arise is that it might be thought now that I have said that we don't need to bother about the others. We do, but what we need to do with them is something very practical: to give and to share and to agitate for more of our national income to be given to the world's needy.

Now for the word "today". I want to remind you if you did not know that the people to whom Christ said this were paid by the day and did not know whether tomorrow they would have a job. They did not have a weekly wage or a monthly salary. They had no security beyond the day, and every morning you would see men make for the marketplace, and they would stand there and maybe the owner of a vineyard would come and say "Would you like a job today?"

It was to these people who literally did not know whether they would have any money tomorrow that Jesus dared to say, in effect: just ask for enough for today, for the next twenty-four hours. Indeed, he spoke of people who had so little that when they came to the end of the day the larder was empty, and if a visitor called they had nothing to set before them and would have to go to a neighbour, saying "I've had a visitor arrive, could you lend me some bread, have you got any left over?" It was to people on the bread line who were paid a small sum by the day for their work that Jesus dared to say: why do you worry about what you are going to eat, and what you are going to drink, and what you are going to put on. If he said it to them, how dare we ever worry about the material needs of life? Jesus could teach people who did not know if they would have a dinner tomorrow not to worry, the heavenly Father would look after that, they needed only to ask him.

One of the most amazing statements in the Bible I have ever come across is in Psalm 37. It is King David speaking and he says this, and when I first read it I'm afraid I said, "That's not true, I'm sure it's not true," but this is what he said: "I have been young and now I am old, and yet I have never seen the righteous forsaken or his children begging bread." The righteous in the Bible are those who are right with God and seeking his righteousness, and then they get the other things added to them. That is a claim which David makes which now, having lived a bit longer, I believe to be true. If man is right with God, and doing what is right by God, and seeking his righteousness, he will not beg for bread.

Of course, sometimes that is really tested and I will confess that there has only been one time in my life when that was really tested with me – when I didn't have anything and didn't know where the next meal was coming from. I thank God I went through that experience, though it didn't last too long, but it was a wonderful experience because I proved it to be true – that if you live twenty-four hours at a time he does provide and he gives you what you need for the next day, and you go on.

Now the word "give". This acknowledges a number of things but I am just going to underline two. The first is that God is the source of all our food. Every bit of food you have comes from God. Whether it has been sitting in your fridge for three weeks or not, it came from God, and without him you would not have anything to eat. It is very important to remember this when our food doesn't come direct from heaven. There is an interesting passage in Deuteronomy 6 where God says to the people of Israel: "Every morning you go out and collect the manna, and it comes straight from heaven, and you know I gave it, but beware lest when you enter into the land which I am going to give you and when your barns are full and your harvests are plentiful, that you do not forget the Lord your God." Then he says an interesting thing: "Remember that it is God who gives you the strength and the power to get wealth to buy food." In other words, even if we do have the power to get food without praying for it, even if we don't have to go out and scrape manna off our lawns, then at least we can say, "God, behind this meal that I am eating you were there. It is from you."

The second thing the word "give" implies is that you have no *right* to food, it is a sheer gift of God's goodness. What right have I to sit down at a table and eat marmalade made from oranges in Spain, and drink coffee from Brazil, and eat cornflakes made from maize grown on the other side of the Atlantic? What right have I that the whole world should serve me at my breakfast table? The answer is that I have none at all.

I think it is most appropriate that at the beginning of a meal we say grace because the word "grace" means something that you couldn't have bought, that you didn't deserve, and that God gave you even though you didn't deserve it. Perhaps just to say literally one word – "grace" – would be enough to give thanks to God. One of the dangers of saying grace is that you get into a routine and say the same words over and over again. Worse still of course is when you say it only if the children are there or when some of your godly friends are present. I have had some amusing experiences in this area. I remember having a meal and the lady said to the husband, "You say grace, dear." So he did and, when he had finished, their little girl looked up and said, "Daddy, what did you do that for?" My grandfather once went to a home for Sunday lunch and the wife did the same thing and landed the husband in it. He started off with the Lord's Prayer, he got into the twenty-third Psalm, and then he had a bit from a comic that he remembered, and he went round and round in circles! Just say thank you! Food is a gift of grace, and if God was not a God of grace we wouldn't have anything to eat. The word "give" reminds you that it is a gift – not a right that you have earned but a sheer gift of his goodness.

If I say "give us today our daily bread", that does not excuse certain other things. It gives me no excuse for idleness. I know that the Israelites had manna from heaven. That was the only way they could get food in the wilderness, but when they got into Canaan they had to dig and plough and work. One of the most astonishing texts in the New Testament is: "If a man will not work, neither shall he eat" (see 2 Thessalonians 3:10). In other words, this is not a by-passing of our need to work if we can work. Nor does it justify carelessness and wastefulness. Because God supplies, we should regard ourselves as stewards of the food.

I think this is one of the lessons in the Gospel account where Jesus said, "Now gather up the fragments that remain." What would be done with those? They would supply the disciples with their next meal. It was the disciples' twelve baskets that got filled, and Jesus showed that we are not to waste food even when it is plentifully supplied by God, nor is it an excuse for gluttony. What somebody has called digging our grave with a knife and fork is not compatible with this prayer. We are not excused in that area, and that is one of the deadly sins according to the book of Proverbs.

We are to eat to live, not to live to eat. It is one of the disturbing features of our contemporary society that some of the most popular programmes on television are designed for gourmets. To say "give us today our daily bread" is to ask God for enough simple good food to help you go on serving him for another twenty-four hours. That is all we are taught to ask – no more, no less – and God has promised to supply no more, no less.

I cannot conclude without spiritualising a bit. There is a connection with Christ. He drew it when he said, "I am the bread of life. Your fathers ate manna in the wilderness, yes but there is a bread that you need if you are going to go on living." Ordinary bread can only keep you going until the end of this life, and then it can't keep you alive and you have got to die. But Jesus said that you need a bread from God that you can eat and live forever.

They said, "Give us this bread, where can we get bread like that?" He said, "You can get it right here from me." He had given them the other sort of bread, and that kept them going another twenty-four hours. If they would come and let him feed them, he could keep them going forever. Jesus is the bread of life. So we are told to look up. We still need bread from heaven: not for our daily meals but for eternal life.

In Luke 14 Jesus gave us a beatitude, which I have never preached on and which I have never heard preached on, which I have never heard quoted in any pulpit anywhere, but it is a beautiful beatitude: "Blessed is he who shall eat bread in the kingdom of God."

FORGIVE US OUR DEBTS
AS WE HAVE FORGIVEN

We call this the "Lord's Prayer" but it is a prayer he never used himself and which he could not have used, and we now come to the petition in the Lord's Prayer that the Lord could never have said, which in the traditional version was: "Forgive us our trespasses as we forgive them that trespass against us." He could have used the second half of that phrase because even when they spat on him and laughed at him and drove nails through his flesh he said, "Father forgive them for they know not what they do." He could not have said the first part of the petition because it was the unanimous testimony of friend and foe alike that Jesus was without sin. He never needed to say "forgive me" because he was the spotless Son of God.

The closer you live to the Lord Jesus the more you feel that you must say, every day, "forgive us our trespasses" or "forgive us our debts". Indeed it is those who have got really close to him who say "Depart from me for I am a sinful man, O Lord." Again we recall that this prayer is for our private use. "Give us this day" implies that we use it (or at least this model) every day.

This tells us a number of things about true prayer. Here is the first: *true prayer must always include the word "forgive" as well as the word "give"*. That may sound pretty elementary, but if you analyse your prayers you may find that you use the word "give" far more than you use the word "forgive": give me this, give me that, give me health, give me comfort, give me money, give me peace, give me joy, give me, give me.... But a good prayer will always go on from "give" to "forgive". This tells us also that we are to bring to God the needs of our soul, as well as the needs of our body, and after having asked "give me" for my body we ask "forgive me" for my soul. It tells me also that I must constantly remember that what I desire and what I deserve are two opposite things. When I say "give me" I must remind myself immediately that I do not deserve to be given that thing.

Therefore when I say "give" I do not deserve it so I must say "forgive" straight away afterwards. Then it tells me that I ought to be thinking of my obligation to God as my heavenly Father, not just his obligation to me. If he is my heavenly Father he has an obligation to feed me and clothe me. That is why I need not worry about what I eat or drink or put on – because he is under an obligation. As a Father he has claimed me and adopted me as his son, so it is now his obligation to feed and clothe his children and I can claim that. But if I only think of his obligations to me as my Father, and not of mine to him, then it is a very one-sided prayer. My obligation to him is to live a holy life as he is holy, and to live a perfect life as he is perfect, and therefore I will need to say "forgive".

This is the only petition with a condition attached to it, and many people have difficulties over this condition. Some of these difficulties are intellectual ones, and I am going to deal with these and I hope I won't put you off by so doing, but my understanding of this phrase is that I have far more practical difficulties than I have intellectual ones. My sympathies are with the lady who was heard muttering as she went out of church, "I'd like to see our vicar love my neighbour" – but I can understand fully the practical difficulties in this prayer.

There are certain intellectual difficulties. A group of aerodynamic experts once sat down and listened to one of their number prove conclusively, mathematically, on a board with figures, that a bumblebee cannot fly. While he was creating all the difficulties with his figures the bumblebees were out getting honey. One of the problems of discussing intellectual difficulties in the pulpit is that some people say: "Well, I never knew those difficulties exist, I just used to pray this prayer."

The phrase "forgive us" presents a psychological difficulty to some Christians. Some think it is bad for Christians to pray "forgive us our sins". They say it will breed an inferiority complex or a guilt complex, that they will always be digging around in their own soul for their sins and become more and more ridden with fears before God. What they maintain you ought to do is get them away from all their sense of guilt and into joy and a peace that never thinks of sin and thinks more of salvation.

A *theological* difficulty is this: I have met Christians who said they did not think we ought to use the Lord's Prayer because when they came to Christ all their sins were forgiven, past and (they think) future, and so they were finished with that and could glory in it for the rest of their lives. I have heard the old Church of England services criticised because they were worded as being uttered by "miserable sinners" asking for forgiveness, and the suggestion is that if you are a Christian you should not start there. You have been forgiven so don't ask for it, and don't go back to where you started.

Another theological difficulty comes from those who believe in what is sometimes called "entire sanctification", which John Wesley believed and taught. I don't think that the Methodists now believe it, but it went from the early Methodists to certain holiness movements and certain Pentecostal groups. These would say that there can come a day in your life when you are entirely sanctified, after which you can be free from sin – and therefore you will not need the Lord's Prayer.

Let me begin by saying that I think the Lord's Prayer was given to the disciples to follow Christ, so to say that we are finished with it doesn't really fit. He didn't give it to the crowds, he called his disciples to him, they said "Teach us to pray" and he was telling them how to do it. So I take it that he gave the Lord's Prayer to us who are following him as his disciples.

Now there are two extremes that I think we need to avoid. One is the idea that there will never be any more need for confession or forgiveness in the Christian's life. I think that is an extreme view which you won't find in the Bible. It is to Christians that the apostle John writes: "If we confess our sins he is faithful and just to forgive us our sins and to cleanse us from all unrighteousness." So it is extreme to say that once you become a Christian your sins are forgiven, you're finished – no more confession, no more forgiveness.

The other extreme I have met is an extraordinary one. I am reminded of it by a lady who gave her testimony thus: "I have been converted five times now," she said, "and each time has been better than the last." Listening to her testimony she seemed to be in and out of salvation between each Sunday and the next. Each day she was so bothered about sins that if she sinned once on Monday she thought she was no longer a Christian. So then she confessed it and she was a Christian by the Monday evening ,and then Tuesday she was out again! In out; in out, she didn't know where she was, and she had no assurance that she was God's child.

So those are two extremes, neither of which is biblical. On the one hand there are those who say, "I'm finished with sins altogether since I became a Christian; I don't need to keep coming back as a miserable sinner," and there are those who are at the other end and say, "I never know whether I'm a Christian or not because I sinned yesterday and that undid all the good work, and I have got to start again." Neither of these is the biblical position.

Let me take you into the Upper Room – where a lot of our questions are sorted out. Jesus took a towel and said, "Peter, I want to wash your feet" and Peter tried at first to refuse. Jesus said "If I don't wash you we can't be friends." He literally said, "You can have no part with me," which means: "We can't have fellowship together." So then Peter swung to the other extreme and said "Well, wash me all over please." Jesus gently told him that he didn't need washing all over now, he been washed, but there was the dirt he picked up on his feet. Jesus wanted to clean that to keep the fellowship between them. I think he was saying something about this very issue. A Christian who has been born again and come to Christ has been washed all over and the symbol of that is baptism, most appropriately – washing from head to toe. They have been washed clean, they are clean through the word of God, but as they walk through life they are going to be picking dirt up on their feet. They will need a daily washing, and Jesus is saying: I want to wash your feet, let me do so – if I don't wash your feet we can't be friends, we can't have fellowship.

In other words, what I am saying is that if a Christian sins (as Christians do) and doesn't get that forgiven, they will lose their fellowship with the Lord. They lose their joy in prayer, their life of worship, their desire to share Christ with other people. It is this that Jesus was bothered about and it is this that the Lord's Prayer is about: a daily cleansing to keep your fellowship with the Lord pure and sweet and clean.

There are five words that the New Testament uses for sin, and they come in two groups: there are two words very like each other and three words very like each other. The first word is "anomia" which means sheer lawlessness. Someone who doesn't recognise any rules for life, who just plays the fool and does what he wants is lawless. The second word is *parabasis* which means "to step over" or trespass, to step over a line. Think of a fence with a sign saying "Keep out", and you climb over it. You have trespassed into forbidden territory.

Now I am going to point out something that will cause you to sit up and think. Neither of these two words is ever used in the scriptures in the Lord's Prayer. It is assumed that Christians will not be deliberately lawless and will not deliberately and maliciously go where they ought not to go. This is not what we ask for, and it is a tragedy that the word "trespass" ever got into the Lord's Prayer. It is not there.

The third word is *hamartia*, which as in archery means to miss your mark, to fall short of the target. That is a word that is used in the Lord's Prayer.

The fourth word is *paraptoma*, which means to fall as on an icy road, to slip when you did not intend to slip, accidentally to do something that you had no intention of doing.

The fifth and the last word which comes in this very passage, Matthew 6, that we are taking is *opheilema* and that means your debts, what you owe. It is this word that is used in the Lord's Prayer. The word "debts" is a far better translation because it is not trespassing that we are thinking about, it is falling short of our target and it is owing God something, not having done what we should have done. Indeed this forgiveness is for what we call sins of omission rather than sins of commission.

If I may quote the Book of Common Prayer, it means precisely this: we have left undone those things which we ought to have done. Is there any Christian who would dare get up and say: "I get to the end of the day without needing to say 'I have left undone the things I ought to have done'"? Is it not true that the nearer you get to Christ, the more you think of the things that you might have said, the letters you might have written, the people you might have visited instead of watching television. The more you look at your life the more you realise the things you didn't do.

That this part of the Lord's Prayer is not as much concerned with the bad things you did as the good things you didn't do puts a different complexion on it. This can spoil your friendship with God. He wanted you to do that thing, he wanted you to write that letter, he wanted you to go and cheer that person up, he wanted you to go and tell someone about Christ – and you didn't do it, and you owed him that. Jesus is telling us to get our debts paid.

You could set your clock by my great grandfather – he went around the village at five o'clock on Saturday evening paying all his debts. He would never enter the Lord's day a penny in debt. They would always say, "There goes old Pawson, paying his debts." Now we are to do that every day with God. Get the accounts straight with him and go to bed straight.

We can go a little further than this. Jesus once told a parable about a servant who was ploughing a field or minding sheep and who came in and who was then going to sit down, but his master said, "Bring my meal first." So the servant had to go on and bring the meal. You might have said, "Well, that's really adding insult to injury. He has worked hard all day, now you make him get the meal." Then Jesus said "Do you think that servant should be thanked for doing that extra thing for his master? No, because when he has done all he is commanded he has only done his duty. Likewise, you also when you have done what you have been commanded have only done your duty, you are still, when you have done your best, unprofitable servants." I underline that word "unprofitable". When I have done my best for God I get to the end of the day in debt to God for what I haven't done.

I am still unprofitable. He has still done more for me than he ever got back from me, and I am still in debt and I need to pray about this. 1 John teaches us that if anyone says he hasn't got this, he deceives himself. I might add that such a person doesn't deceive anyone else.

The second phrase that has caused difficulty to people is "as we forgive" and the difficulty I can express like this: is not the gospel of Christ free forgiveness, free grace, no conditions, no bargains, no contracts? Doesn't God say that if you repent and believe you are forgiven? Yet here we are in the Lord's Prayer being told to do something for someone else before God will forgive us. Is this not salvation by good works? Isn't this God going right against the principle of free grace and saying, "I won't forgive you your sins until you have been out and done something for someone else"? Is that not bargaining? Is it not putting a condition to forgiveness?

Again I begin by affirming that this is not about our first conversion. This prayer is not a prayer for the unbeliever and it was never meant to be. It is a prayer for the Christian, for the believer, every day. What then does the condition mean? Does it mean that God has laid down a kind of law that unless we pass forgiveness on he won't forgive us? Is it a kind of spiritual law of the universe that the positive lead that comes to us from God doesn't produce any current unless the negative earth is earthed in my neighbour? Is that what is meant? I have heard many sermons say that.

I don't think it is that God can't forgive you under these conditions. I think it is simply that he won't. The real reason why he doesn't forgive those Christians who don't forgive others is very simple: he doesn't feel like it. It is the feelings of God that matter. Now before you really wonder what I am saying, let me tell you where I found it. I found it in the parable in which Jesus said, "A king in his generosity and pity forgave a man three hundred pounds," and then he heard that that man went out and flung a fellow man into jail for a much smaller sum. The king was angry and said: "I take back my forgiveness." The words of Jesus teach how God feels about your unforgivingness.

God is my Father so I know how he feels because I am a father. If your children were come to you and say "Daddy, can I have a sweet" and you gave a sweet to each of them, and then you were to find that one of them had stolen the sweets from the others and went and had eaten all the sweets, and then had the cheek to come back and say "Can I have another sweet?" you would say, "You're not getting another sweet from me, I'm very cross with you."

Why would you be angry because one of the children did this? There's a very simple reason: because you don't want your child to to grow up like that, and if you were to go on indulging a child behaving badly he would grow up naughty, selfish, a thief. God wants us to grow up to be more like him, and he wants us to be forgiving as he is forgiving. If he were to forgive you each day your debts and you were not forgiving others, he would be encouraging you to go on behaving like that, and he is not that kind of a Father. He would be cross with you, and if you are not prepared to forgive others their debts then he is not going to forgive yours. He would be angry.

Now I can understand that – it makes sense in this context, God is just telling us how he feels about us, and he is talking about his children, believers, Christians. Do you expect him to go on wiping out your debts if you don't wipe out others' debts? If he were to go on doing that, he would be doing you harm. He is not indulging your sin – he would be destroying your character, and he is not that kind of a Father. I thank God that my earthly father wouldn't have let me get away with this, and I thank my heavenly Father that he doesn't either.

God stated what his feelings are and I can see his reasons

for it. An unforgiving person does not know what he is asking for when he says "forgive". An unforgiving person will not appreciate forgiveness even if he gets it. An unforgiving person will be made more unforgiving if he is forgiven under those circumstances.

God's will is for us to grow up to be more like him. Tennyson put it like this: "Forgive him seventy times and seven, for all the blessed souls in heaven are both forgiving and forgiven." In other words, be like your heavenly Father. God will not forgive your debts at the end of each day if you are not learning to be like him. Otherwise, it would not be good fathering, it would be bad discipline.

General Oglethorpe was a civil servant whom John Wesley approached on behalf of a convict, to plead for him. Oglethorpe said to Wesley, "I never forgive." John Wesley quietly said to him: "Then I hope, sir, that you never sin." This is what it is about. I can sum this up in two words: forgiving; forgiven. That is the law for Christians. Now the practical difficulties with this are not intellectual. They are in the heart, not in the head. Augustine called this petition in the Lord's Prayer "the terrible petition".

A modern scholar has said of all the petitions in the Lord's Prayer this is the most frightening. Robert Louis Stevenson who led his family in family prayers every day and always finished with the Lord's Prayer, once at breakfast time, in the middle of family prayers, got up and walked out of the dining room. His wife went out to him and said, "What's the matter, Robert?" He replied, "I'm not fit to pray that prayer today." "Why?" she asked. He then told her about a resentment, a malice that had been brooding in his heart since the previous day. He said, "I can't pray that prayer today. It's easy enough to say 'Give us this day our daily bread,' there are no conditions attached. God will give us that for the asking, but here he says, 'I can't give you this for the asking, not unless...' and if I am praying this prayer while I'm nursing grudges, bitterness, resentment, jealousy, then I am literally asking God not to forgive my debts and that's a terrible prayer."

I came across this in Mrs Gaskell's book *Sylvia's Lovers*. Sylvia refuses to forgive the man who brought about her father's condemnation as a criminal (and he was a criminal) and his execution. A lady says to Sylvia, "It said in the Bible, Sylvia, that we are to forgive." She replies, "There's some things I know I never forgive and there's other's I can't, and I won't either." "But Sylvia you pray to be forgiven your trespasses as you forgive them that trespass against you." Sylvia then says, "Well, if I'm to be taken at my word I'll not pray at all, that's all. It's well enough for them that has but little to forgive to use them words. I tell you my flesh and blood wasn't made for forgiving and forgetting ... when I love I love, when I hate I hate, and him who has done harm to me or to mine I may keep from striking or murdering but I'll never forgive."

That is a very human passage but a tragic one because it finds an echo in our hearts and because forgiveness is not just a matter of avoiding doing any harm to someone, it is positively going to them and re-establishing relationships.

I once went to a woman whom I knew was not speaking to another woman in the church and said, "Can't you forgive her what she did?" She said "I have done. I'm not speaking to her any more but I have forgiven her." I replied, "You haven't forgiven her. Don't call that forgiveness." "Well," she said, "I'm not going to do her any harm and I'm not going to say a thing against her." But she still wouldn't say a thing to her, and that is not forgiveness.

I find this very hard. It is a rare and beautiful thing when you see human beings forgive each other. I remember reading of a businessman who went out to India with his young wife. He travelled all around India on business while she stayed in Calcutta. He got into wrong ways, and he got into trouble with women and crooks, and he wrecked his life. She wondered what was wrong and kept asking why he looked so worried and why he was losing weight. He wouldn't tell her, just saying that he was busy.

Then one day he couldn't stand it any longer and told her the whole sordid story. She staggered back against the wall as if he had struck her with a whip. He said: "For the first time in my life I saw love crucified by sin." Then, and this is the point of the story, she did a beautiful thing. She came and put her arms around his neck and said, "We'll put this right together." Now that is real forgiveness, a rare and beautiful thing.

I remember seeing it in Berlin. There I met Betty Elliott whose husband was murdered by the Auca Indians. She was walking along arm in arm with two Auca Indians who had murdered her husband and made her a widow, and since they didn't know anything about Western civilisation and had come straight from the jungle she was teaching them how to use a knife and fork, how to go to the toilet – all the kinds of things that they needed to be taught – like little children. That is the practical difficulty of forgiveness. How does a woman like that teach and help her husband's murderers?

So that is the practical difficulty of saying, "As we forgive...." It is not intellectual difficulties that stop someone from saying the Lord's Prayer, it is this. The other practical difficulty is with the phrase "forgive us". I don't know if you ever realised how difficult it is for God to forgive you. With us, if I can't forgive my neighbour it is my pride, it is myself, my reputation, my rights, and I have got to crucify self to forgive the other person, but with God it is not that. It's not pride. Why does God find difficulty? I'll tell you: because of his purity, because of his holiness, because of his goodness. He just cannot bear sin at all. He hates it.

How does he get round the difficulty of my debts? By paying them for me. That is the only thing that makes it possible for God to forgive my debts. The word "forgive" in the Hebrew language means two things. It means to remit a debt and it also means to pay it, and the same word does for both. In the Middle East if you are in debt, your debts are written up on a sheet of paper and they are pinned up in the marketplace for everyone to see. That is an added incentive to get them paid quickly, but if a man is willing to pay your debt and remit it for you, he will come along and fold it over, put a nail through it and write his own name across the sheet of paper, and your debts are done with.

In Colossians 2:14 Paul says that God has in Christ taken the bond of debts, which was written against us and nailed it to the cross. He has finished it and written across it the name of Jesus. "Forgive us our debts" – it is as difficult for God to forgive us as it is for us to forgive others, but the practical difficulties were resolved at the cross and every act of forgiveness is written in the blood of Jesus.

Finally, is there anything like the joy of forgiveness, of knowing that it is over and done with, knowing that the person who has forgiven you will never mention it again, knowing that they love you, that they will give you the fatted calf, the ring on your finger, the shoes on your feet, the robe on your back, and bring you home – that is forgiveness. "Forgive us our debts" – all that we owe to you every day.

LEAD US NOT INTO TEMPTATION
BUT DELIVER US
FROM THE EVIL ONE

I don't suppose I will ever have the opportunity, but I have found myself musing on the possibility on my ever being invited to Buckingham Palace to talk to the Queen, and thinking that if that ever did arise, the very first concern I would have would be to get hold of someone who could tell me how to behave and what to say – someone who was accustomed to meeting her and who would tell me when to say "Your Majesty" and when to say "Ma'am" and all the rest of it, and how you come into her presence and how you talk to her – and if there is something you would like to ask her to do, how you set about doing that. I suppose again (still musing) the best person to help me here would be Prince Charles, and if he would say, "All right, I'm used to her, I'll tell you how to come into her presence and what to say", then I should be very grateful to him. This may seem a rather silly way to begin, yet I want to remind you that whenever you pray you are coming to the throne of the universe and to the King of kings.

It would be very wrong if we rushed into God's presence without bothering to ask: how do you come to God? What do you say when you meet him? The amazing thing is that his own Son has taught us how to address him, how to present a petition to him when you come into his royal presence. The Lord's Prayer is nothing less than the very Prince of peace telling us how to approach his Father. That is why we are studying the Lord's Prayer, lest we rush rudely into the presence of God and blurt out words without realising to whom we have come and what we ought to be saying.

Now the first rule of etiquette when you approach the throne of heaven is to talk about what God wants before you talk about what you want. Yet in so many of our prayers we rush in with our shopping list before we even begin to think: what would *he* like me to pray about? So the Lord's Prayer tells us to pray for three things for God before you bring any of your own. We are to pray that his name may be honoured and hallowed, to pray that his kingdom may come, to pray that his will may be done – that these three things of reverence, allegiance and obedience might be seen among us. But having said that, it is then our great privilege to bring our needs, and there are three basic needs which I have every day of life. I need food. I need forgiveness. I need freedom.

These are the three basic needs of everyone on earth, every single twenty-four hours: food for the body, forgiveness for my sin, and freedom for my soul. Now why freedom? That word doesn't occur in the Lord's Prayer. I use it because there is only one real kind of freedom. I have heard freedom defined in many ways. President Roosevelt defined it as freedom from want, freedom from fear, freedom to work and freedom to worship. That may be a fine definition but it is not the Bible's one. Then there are those who say real freedom is freedom from war, freedom from famine, freedom from disease, freedom from hunger – that kind of thing. There are many who campaign for that kind of freedom. Then there are others who say freedom is freedom from authority, freedom not to be told what to do, freedom from the establishment, freedom from convention. There are many people today confusing that with real freedom.

Then there are those who think that freedom is freedom to do wrong, freedom to do exactly what one wants to do, freedom to do what I like, but that is not freedom, it is sheer slavery. When someone has done that for some years they are a slave. They know no freedom. I remember two drunks on the top of a bus who were discussing the reception they would get from their wives when they got home. One was clearly preparing his speech and he was trying it out on the other. He was saying, "Well, when I see her and she sees me, I'll say 'I'm free, aren't I?'" But he wasn't free. He was a poor chained little man. Real freedom is the freedom to do right. That is the only real freedom there ever is. It is this freedom which we need to pray for every twenty-four hours of life. This is a prayer for Christians, and this is a freedom that Christians will not have unless they pray for it daily: "Deliver us from evil." That is real freedom. When someone is free from the chains of their own bad habits and can break the bad things that in their finer moments they regret, when someone can throw off the chains of their past and live as they know they were meant to live – then that person is free and nobody can chain them. Others may put them in prison, and they may even face martyrdom, but such a person is free to do what is right.

That is the freedom the Bible offers. It doesn't offer you the freedom to do wrong because that is slavery and bondage. It offers you the freedom to do right, deliverance from evil. Now I am afraid that this phrase has caused much division of opinion – especially the first half of this petition, "Lead us not into temptation...." I have found the most incredible variety in translations. Here are some of them: "keep us clear of temptation", "do not bring us to the test", "do not let us be subjected to temptation", "do not bring us to a testing which is beyond our power to withstand", "don't bring us to breaking point", "guide us away from temptation", "spare us from the testing which is beyond our strength".

The real difficulty is this: surely the Bible states clearly God never tempts anyone. How then can we ask him not to do something that he never would do anyway?

Where do temptations come from? They come from three sources only. They may come from the flesh or the world or the devil, but most certainly not from God. You were never tempted by God in your life and you never will be. By the word "flesh" I don't just mean the body. I mean this body and the habits I built into it before I knew Christ. I mean the old me. I mean the person I was before he set me free.

Old habits come back and the old weaknesses reappear sometimes years after your conversion. It would be dishonest of any Christian to get up and say "I am now beyond temptation" because it is not true. The old flesh still hangs around. It is dead but won't lie down, and that troubles us.

The world is the second source. I mean by that the society around us, the advertisements that shoot their messages at us, the habits of people we work with, the way of living of people next door. This is what I mean by the world, which is the second source.

The third source is the devil himself. Shouldn't we be praying about one of these three sources of temptation?

Again I hope that I am not going to raise problems that were not in your mind to begin with. If they weren't, then forget them. But I know that this problem may be in your mind. Let me just put in a little hint that might help. The word translated "temptation" is a word in the Greek language which actually means two different things. It can either be translated "tempt" or "test". In the Greek language the same word does for the two things and either can mean a good thing or a bad thing.

To test someone is not necessarily a bad thing. It is good because when you test a person you are hoping he will pass and succeed – and become a stronger and a better person. Why do we have driving test? A test is to stop people doing wrong and this same word can be used for the word "test". Indeed the New English Bible has "Do not bring us to the test". So is that the meaning? There is no doubt about it that God does test his people. In Genesis it says that he tested Abraham, and there is no mention of the devil in that chapter. It was God testing Abraham, and Abraham came through the test with flying colours. He was seen to be the great man that he was, in that he was prepared to let go of his son who was very dear to him. He passed the test. Now that is the meaning, and if the New English Bible is right in saying "test" why should we ask to be delivered from tests? It is as if a student in a university is asking to be excused the exams, or as if someone starting to drive asks to be excused the driving test. Why should we pray that we may not be brought to the test? Knowing that when we are tested, and if we come through, we are stronger and better and more clearly sons of God than we were before, James says, "Count it a joy" when these tests come. These trials make you steadfast, and they prove you and they make you a better Christian.

So that I am afraid quite frankly I have to say that I must rule out this good meaning of the word "test" because I don't think we have any right to ask to be delivered from the trials and tests which will prove us and strengthen us. Furthermore if that is what it means it doesn't link up with the second phrase "... but deliver us from evil." It would just make nonsense and become a contradiction. So we have to look further. Quite frankly, I believe you cannot alter the word "temptation". It is "lead us not into temptation". Now there have been many attempts to tone it down. Someone tried to do so by putting an extra comma in: "Lead us, not into temptation, but deliver us from evil" – to make it a prayer for guidance. But I honestly think we can't get around it that way. Then there have been those who have toned it down by saying: "lead us not into it" – signifying the same as "lead us out of...." So we will ask to be led out of temptation and the

Philips translation does this: "keep us clear of temptation". But that is not the prayer, and it seems a roundabout way of saying it. Why did our Lord not tell us to say "lead us out of temptation" if that was what he meant? What he told us to pray is "lead us not into...." I must take this in its simplest, clearest meaning. It does not say "don't tempt us...." That would be wrong.

"Lead us not into temptation" implies two profound truths. One: God *could* lead you into temptation, and two, under certain circumstances God *would* lead you into temptation.

Now I must try to justify those extraordinary statements. If this phrase means what it says, those two things are true. Let me take the first. Would God ever lead anyone into temptation? The answer is that he did. Luke 4 has this statement: "Then Jesus was led by the Spirit into the wilderness to be tempted by the devil." You need go no further than the life of Jesus himself to know that God led his own Son into temptation. He was led by the Spirit of God, not an evil spirit. He was led by the Spirit of God to be tempted by the devil. God had a purpose to be fulfilled. But here is the difference and I must go carefully and slowly so that you are with me all the way. There is a profound difference between God leading Christ into temptation and God leading me in. What is the difference? I cannot take it as well as Christ. Why not? Because I do not come to the devil as someone who has managed to escape his clutches. I come as someone who has already been tempted and fallen. I come into the ring with someone I have already fought and lost. I come to face a person who already knows how to get hold of me. But when Jesus faced the devil he did not know that experience of being tempted to the point of defeat.

Therefore I am praying in this prayer: Lord, you could lead your own Son into temptation, but please don't lead me there. The devil already has something pinned on me. He has already got hold of me and I must not be brought into the ring with him.

But that only brings me to a further problem. Under what circumstances would God do to me what he did to Jesus? In what situations would he lead me into temptation to face the devil? Why would he do this? I must now go to a remarkable passage in 1 Corinthians 5, in which there is an extraordinary phrase. Paul is writing to a church: "It is actually reported that there is immorality among you and a kind that is not even found even among pagans. For a man is living with his father's wife. When you are assembled [that's in your church meeting] my Spirit is present with the power of our Lord Jesus, you are to deliver this man to Satan for the destruction of his flesh that his spirit may be saved in the day of the Lord." There is one of the most surprising statements. If a man in your fellowship were in this kind of immoral situation that was widely known, I think you would probably pray that he may be delivered from Satan. But the New Testament teaches that the best way to deal with him is to deliver him to Satan. Why? Because that is the only way that you will really save his spirit. In other words there is a situation in which you are to be delivered to Satan for your own good. Now let me go even more carefully and slowly here because we are in very deep spiritual truth. What God is saying through Paul here is this: there comes a point where the best way you can help a person is to expose him to temptation. Only in this way will he come to realise his need of getting back to God, and in certain circumstances someone who is playing around with sin should be allowed to go further into it, that he may realise where his road is leading, and come back to God even if it is at the cost of the destruction of his body – if you can save his soul. In other words a dreadful and a dangerous situation needs a drastic remedy.

Can I apply that now to us? When I begin the day without asking God to lead me not into temptation, and to deliver me from evil, I go out into the world quite confident, quite sure that I can deal with every situation, that I can keep pure and clean and that I can live a Christian life. How can God possibly get through to me that I can't? How can he possibly teach me what a fool I am being? There is one way and one way only that God can do that. It is to say: I will lead you into the position where you will find temptation too much for you. It is the only way I will get you back. It is the only way you will see that you just can't go out so confidently and live the life that you were meant to live in your *own* strength.

I know from bitter experience, and I daresay you know this, that when you go out into the day without asking God to protect you from evil you will very rapidly find that temptation is stronger that day than it has been for a long time. You feel the devil is real and you find you are in the middle of a battle. It could be that God has led you into that battle and led you into temptation so that you might realise you are not going to get through the day yourself. It is his drastic way of bringing you back to himself. It is his saying: you have chosen this road, then go down this road until you realise you need me again. So we should begin the day by saying to God: God, please don't deal with me like that today. God, I'm coming at the beginning of the day. I'm asking you to deliver me from evil today so that you don't need to lead me into temptation to teach me a lesson. Just keep me from harm. Deliver me from the evil one.

In other words don't lead me into temptation but do deliver me from the evil one. The "but" makes sense. Don't deal with me that way deal, deal with me this way. I will guarantee that a believer who prays that at the beginning of the day will find that temptations lose their power that day. But I will also guarantee that if you don't start the day like that, temptations will increase in power and it is God's way of disciplining you as his child. I remember one parent telling me that they were trying to stop their child smoking. They tried again and again to forbid it, to punish them, and they got nowhere. So, finally, they hit on the best way. They said, "Here you are. Here's a box of cigars, now just smoke those. Go on, smoke them all." The boy did and he shared them with his friends and they had a lost weekend. He never smoked again. God is our heavenly Father and sometimes he says, "Alright, if you won't learn the easy way to trust me then go down this road. I lead you into temptation. See how you get on without my help and you will soon come back."

So we turn to the second half of this prayer, but before I do perhaps I should mention something else. In 1 Corinthians 10:13 it says: "God is faithful and he will not let you be tempted beyond your strength, but with the temptation will also provide the way of escape that you may be able to endure it." If God led me into temptation without at the same time providing an escape route, then he would be causing me to sin and that would be un-godlike and an unholy thing to do. But God, even when he leads me into temptation, will at the same time follow me with a way of escape so when I realise I need him, at that moment I can get out of that temptation. In other words, God will lead me deeper into temptation but follow me with a way out if I am willing to learn. As soon as I do, I am out of it. But if anybody claims that promise in 1 Corinthians 10:13 as protection against the possibility of sinning, then they should read 1 Corinthians 10:12, the previous verse: "Therefore let anyone who thinks that he stands take heed lest he fall."

It is plain sailing from now on, as we turn to: "But deliver us from evil." Nobody quarrels with this, yet we are not quite through the wood because there is a further problem. There is no such *thing* as evil. Now don't get me wrong. I have not become a Christian Scientist, and I have not accepted the philosophies that deny the reality of wrongdoing. But you can't show me a bundle of evil. *There are only evil persons*. Just as in fact there is no such *thing* as love, there are only loving *persons*. Sometimes we talk as if goodness and badness were things that you could parcel up, that exist apart from people. But they do not. The only evil in the world is to be found in evil persons, and if there were no persons in the world there would be no evil in it. Moreover, if God was not love there would be no love. Love doesn't exist by itself, and evil does not exist by itself. So when we say "deliver us from evil", what do we mean? We do not mean deliver us from something impersonal, from a kind of force around us. It is interesting that Jesus told us to pray: "... deliver us from the evil one". It is not from evil as a vague thing, it is from the evil *one*, the person who embodies evil. Whenever you pray, every day, you should mention Satan in your prayers according to this. You should deliberately pray against the devil when you pray, otherwise you are literally a prey to him. In the Bible, from the very beginning evil is a personal thing. Evil comes to Adam and Eve speaking as a person, and all the way through evil is a person. Somebody has recently said that the devil never did a more effective stroke of work than when he persuaded man to disbelieve in him. Never laugh at the devil. Take him as seriously as our Lord took him. Our Lord took him seriously at the beginning of his ministry and the temptations, and all the way through. He said, "You see this woman, she has been bound by Satan for eighteen years" – and with a word he set her free. All the way through he was saying "Get behind me, Satan". Even when he came to the cross he said: "Now is the prince of this world cast out". I don't think you understand the real situation if you don't believe in a personal devil – not a little black imp but a highly intelligent powerful person who knows you

better than you know him, who is a liar and a slanderer and
a murderer, who is so subtle that you would not recognise
him even if he appeared before you. Sometimes when he
does appear, he appears as an angel of light. Sometimes he
comes to you behind the face of your best friend and you
have to say to that friend, "Get behind me, Satan" as Jesus
said to Peter.

The devil is like a prowling lion. He is a red dragon. He
is a beast. He is a wily serpent. You are no match for him at
all. Jesus said of the devil that he is the god of this world,
the person people really worship. He is the prince of this
world. He is the ruler of this world. The people who are
reading and watching news about the horrors of life in our
world are reading what the ruler of this world is doing with
human lives. The media may not often mention him by name,
but they do sometimes. The newspapers that seem to take a
delight in publicising the weaknesses and sins of mankind
are those which most frequently mention devil worship.

Therefore when I pray "deliver us from the evil one" I
am acknowledging three major truths about our world. Truth
number one: I need to be delivered from Satan. Truth number
two: I cannot deliver myself from Satan. Truth number three:
the Lord can deliver me. Consider the first truth – that I need
to be delivered from Satan. Why? Because I was born in his
kingdom, because my body came into his world, because
from the first time I cried my first cry I was a citizen of the
kingdom of Satan. As I grew up I found it easier to say no
than yes. I found it easier to tell lies than to tell the truth. I
found it easier to be naughty than good. I was brought up in
his kingdom. That is why I need to be delivered from him.
He had me for years, and Christ set me free.

That is why I need to pray to be delivered. I am one of
his old pals. I am one of his old victims. I am one of his old
citizens. Deliver us from the evil one – and because I go on

living in this world and will go on until I am dead, I am not beyond the reach of Satan's control. My body is not beyond his reach. Jesus taught that disease is a work of Satan. I see people lying ill, and they are not beyond the reach of Satan. Nobody is until they are dead. As long as we are living in his world we are within his reach, so every day we need to say: "Deliver us from the evil one." So I acknowledge my need to be delivered from the evil one.

Secondly, I acknowledge that I cannot deliver myself from the evil one. What a fool I am to try! He is more subtle than I am. He is stronger than I am. He is superior to me in every way except that I am a believer, and he knows me so well. He has a brilliant intellect. He can argue with me until I find myself arguing for sin – until I can justify what is wrong. If I think I can tackle him on my own, I cannot – so I must acknowledge that I cannot deliver myself.

But, thirdly, I can be delivered by God in Christ. That is what I acknowledge when I pray this prayer. The Gospels are clear that, in Jesus, Satan met his match – that whenever they clashed head on, Jesus always won. Even at the cross when Satan flung everything he had against Christ, Jesus said, "Now is the prince of this world cast out. I am winning." When he cried, "It is finished" it was a cry of victory, and having spoiled principalities and powers he made a show of them, openly triumphing over them in the cross. There is only one person in the entire history of the human race who has defeated Satan from birth to death, and that one person is Jesus Christ.

I am sorry that Psalm 23 has been so misunderstood. "The valley of the shadow..." is nothing to do with dying. Yet it is said at almost every funeral. The word "death" does not even come in the original Hebrew of Psalm 23. The valley of deep shadow, the valley of darkness, is a valley of *temptation*. It is a valley that you and I will go through this week whether we go through dying or not. You notice that his fear in the valley is not fear of death. He says, "I will fear no evil". Evil is what he fears. Why does he not fear evil? Because the Shepherd is with him. "Your rod, your staff" – with them, God will fight off evil for me. It may be that tomorrow morning you will go through the valley of deep darkness and the temptation will be there. You will come through it without fearing evil because the good Shepherd is with you.

When I pray "deliver us from evil" I am asking that the Lord will be with me through the day. Don't deal with me the hard way, Lord. Don't push me into temptation to teach me a lesson. Don't expose me to Satan. I don't want to learn that way. I want to learn the better way. Deliver us from evil. May your presence be with me in the valley of the shadow. Then I will fear no evil.

The Lord's Prayer begins with God and it ends with Satan. When you pray, you are coming to God. After praying, you are going to face Satan. When you pray you are coming to heaven, but then you are coming down to earth, Satan's kingdom. Therefore as we should pray "Our Father in heaven" we should be aware of the evil one on earth. We come to God to find our needs: food, forgiveness and freedom to do right. Lord, deliver us from evil – and we go out to enjoy the freedom of the sons of God.

ENDING IN PRAISE

There are two reasons why the Bible needs to be constantly re-translated. Firstly, words change their meaning and sometimes even come to mean the opposite of what they meant some centuries ago. Secondly, our knowledge of the original manuscripts improves tremendously over the years because archeologists dig up different early copies of parts of the Bible.

As the copies they dig up go back and back in years, nearer to the time when it was actually written (and we haven't one single original manuscript of the entire Bible), we get more and more accurate versions. We are able to correct the ones we have. Let me hasten to add that in spite of all the corrections translators have been able to make because they have discovered earlier manuscripts, not one item of Christian belief or behaviour has had to be changed as a result. So it really doesn't matter what translation you have, from that point of view. Nevertheless, naturally we do want as accurate a Bible as we can have. Scholars are now convinced that we have the New Testament 98% as it was written. That is an astonishing achievement. There is no other book two thousand years old that we have with that accuracy.

There is still some uncertainty about 2% of the words in the New Testament – so little that we can leave that on one side. But there have been some surprises as we have discovered earlier copies of New Testament writings. Let me mention one or two. It came as a shock to some people to find that the story of the woman taken in adultery in John 8 is not in the earliest copies. In modern translations you may not find it in the text. It came as a surprise to others to find that part of Mark 16 was missing from earlier copies of that Gospel, and you may find that the section concerned is put at the foot of the page. But one of the biggest surprises that came to those who made a study of early copies was that the Lord's Prayer does not contain the phrase: "... yours is the kingdom, the power, and the glory, for ever and ever. Amen."

I was tempted to finish this study with the phrase "... lead us not into temptation but deliver us from the evil one." But having thought it over, I am going to go on and complete the Lord's Prayer as you know it.

This raises three questions: when was this phrase added, where did it come from, and why was it put in? I think we shall find that when we have answered those three questions we will want to study it.

First of all, when was it added? The answer is within the first hundred years after the death and resurrection of Jesus Christ. In some of the earliest Christian books the Lord's prayer is written out with the phrase at the end, even though it is not there in the Gospels of Matthew or Luke.

So where did this closing phrase come from? Did somebody sit down and write it? Did a committee get together to try and improve the church services and decide on a liturgical basis to improve the Lord's Prayer? The answer is that it came from the only scriptures the early Christians had – the Old Testament. It was from 1 Chronicles 29. Read the prayer of David and see if you can spot this phrase: "Blessed art thou O Lord the God of Israel, our Father for ever and ever. Thine O Lord is the greatness and the power and the glory and the victory and the majesty for all that is in the heavens and in the earth is thine. Thine is the kingdom O Lord." Do you notice that it is all there?

It looks as if the early Christians, reading that prayer of David, thought that was a perfect ending for prayer and they tagged it on to the Lord's Prayer and it has been said ever since by Christians in the East and the West, by Roman and Protestant. Churches all over the world have included this final phrase.

Why was it added? Some people suggest: to make the prayer a bit longer. There are those who think that a prayer is not really a prayer if they don't pray for a long time, and for them the Lord's Prayer can seem much too short! You can get through it too quickly. But I don't think that is the reason at all.

Then there are those who felt that it was added to round it off nicely, just as you round off a letter: yours sincerely or yours faithfully. Again, I don't think that was it. Though I did come across a Christmas prayer in the Book of Common Prayer, in which the petition itself is only one very short sentence and two-thirds of the Collect is a conclusion: "through the same our Lord Jesus Christ who liveth and reigneth with thee in the same Spirit, ever one God, world without end. Amen." That conclusion is two-thirds of the prayer. So did they add the final phrase simply to round off the Lord's Prayer? No. Did they do it because they didn't like finishing with the devil? I told you that the Lord's Prayer begins with "Our Father" and ends with mention of "the evil one". Was it that Christians didn't like to finish thinking about Satan and wanted to get back to God again? Maybe. I will tell you why I think it was, but I have no evidence. The phrase "yours is the kingdom, the power, the glory, forever and ever. Amen" is not prayer, it is *praise*.

It is a response to God of praise. It is not asking for a single thing. It is saying: Lord, before I finish praying I want to praise you, I want to tell you how wonderful I think you are. I want to stop asking for things now and I want to let my heart fill up with praise, thinking of your greatness. I think that is why it came. I think the reason the Lord Jesus didn't tell them to say it is that this praise has to come spontaneously from the heart. You can teach a person to pray but you can't teach them to praise. Praise must come as a response. I think the Lord told them what to pray for, but left Christians to praise and to find out how to praise his name. They found out with the words of David, and thought: that is how we would like to praise him.

So the Lord's Prayer as we use it today doesn't finish on a note of prayer but on a note of praise: yours is the kingdom, the power, and the glory. That is only my guess. You can reject it. You can accept your own guess if you have got a better one, but I am sticking with that one for now. There are three things we say in this praise: yours is the kingdom; yours is the power; yours is the glory. I see in those three statements a statement of faith, a statement of hope and a statement of love. You would not say the first unless you were a person of faith in God. You wouldn't say the second unless you were a person of hope in God. You certainly wouldn't say the third unless you were a person who loves God. Let us then look at these three phrases in that light. To say yours is the *kingdom* is the most amazing statement. It is a most difficult statement for reason to accept because the facts seem to be against it. What does it mean? I'm going to put it in rather crude English. It means: "O God, you're boss, you're in charge, you're in the control room of the universe. You arrange everything." Can you look at the world as we know it and say: yours is the kingdom, you are on the throne? A little girl went to a church women's meeting with her mother and listened to the choruses, then started singing her own: "God is still on the phone, God is still on the phone"! Now that is tremendous, but if God is only on the phone and not on the throne then what is the point of praying? If God is only on the phone then he can give us sympathy but not succour. He can say, "Well I'm very sorry for you but I really can't do anything about it either, but I do give you my sympathy." What is the point of asking God to give me my daily bread if he is not on the throne and not in charge? What is the point of asking God to control my life and deliver me from Satan if God is not in control? It is the basis of the whole prayer.

Either God is king or he is not, and if he is not then there is no point in praying. Why do some people seem unable to say this? First, because you cannot see visibly his methods of control. You can't see how God connects up with events. You can see events and say: "Was God in that or not?" A further reason is that many of the things that happen seem to be contrary to his purpose and his will. There are things in nature and human affairs which seem so contradictory that people wonder whether God is in control.

But the Christian, at the end of his prayer, affirms his faith and in effect declares: in spite of all that I see, you are on the throne (yours is the kingdom), therefore I pray because prayer will change things as you really are in charge. Do all this that I have asked for – you are on the throne. So it is a tremendous step of faith to say that God reigns.

The second statement is equally a step of faith: yours is the *power*. Now we have been through many different ages: ice age, Stone Age, Bronze Age, iron age, the atomic age. But I think the name that ought to be given to this present age is the Power Age. Mankind has had power in its hands in my lifetime as man never had before. We are harnessing the powers of the universe around us. We are harnessing the sun, the tides, oil and many other resources and commodities. We talk about great world powers, power blocs, the corridors of power. There are military powers, financial powers, ideological powers, technological powers. It is like a giant

Pandora's box somebody has opened and let the powers out – and we are afraid. Why? The answer is: because we do not think people are capable of handling such power properly. Lord Acton's much misquoted saying comes in here: "Power tends to corrupt, and absolute power tends to corrupt absolutely." If someone is given tremendous power it can go to his head. It can make him become a dictator. It can make him think he is god. One of my favourite texts, on which I preached in a communist country where some people had great power over their fellow men, was Psalm 62:11 – "Once God has spoken, twice have I heard this, that power belongs to God." That is a tremendous text in the age of nuclear power. Real power is God's power.

What does the text mean? Two things. It means first that all the powers that man is using are resources which God gave us. God packed the atom. God lit the sun. One day we must render our account to God for how we have used the powers he gave us, and we have used most of the power we discovered to blast people into eternity. But the other thing it means is something else. It is not only that the power *of* man is from God, but power *over* man is God's. Man can control some things, but who can control man? God can. God has the power to destroy and to create. He has the power to do things for people and with people that no-one else has the power to do. So this is a statement of hope that the world is in the hands of a power greater than man has.

People sometimes tell me that they are afraid history is going to end when someone presses the wrong button. I say I am not afraid of that even if it were going to happen but I don't believe it will. God has his finger on the button. It is God's power that will bring the world to an end, not man's power. Power belongs to God. Men cannot bring the world to an end. So: "*yours* is the power...." I think of that tremendous scene when Jesus stood before Pilate, and

Pilate was already showing signs of nervousness, asking: "Why don't you answer me? Don't you know I have the power to kill you or set you free?" Jesus calmly said, "You would have no power against me unless it were given you from above." That is also the calm of a Christian who says the Lord's Prayer. That can say to anything: "You have no power against me unless it's given you from God."

Finally: yours is the *glory*. Now "glory" is a word that has gone out of use. A friend of mine went into a secondary school and wrote the word "glorification" on the board to see if any of the pupils had any idea what it meant. He said, "What does that mean?" A hand went up, "It's a shampoo, sir." That was the only answer he could get. What is glorification? The very word "glory" is going out, so let me try and put it again in simpler, perhaps cruder English. "Limelight" is a good equivalent because glory always has about it light, and instead of saying giving someone the glory nowadays we might talk about giving them the limelight. That is getting near the meaning: giving them the credit, giving them the publicity. All this is in the word "glory", and we even talk about basking in reflected glory when we mean that we share a bit of the credit or the publicity. So what we are saying here is: give God the credit.

In Westminster Abbey there is a very interesting memorial which names the famous man it commemorates in about three lines at the top of the stone. The rest of the stone is devoted to describing the man who paid to have it put up! It is a description of this unknown character who was simply climbing on the bandwagon of the famous person. There it is, everything this little man had ever done, and three-quarters of the stone is taken up by his pinching the glory of (I think) a great soldier.

I am afraid that even in our Christian service we can do this. God is a jealous God and he will not share his glory with another. If we make too much of a Pope or an evangelist or a preacher or singer, then we are doing what this prayer and this praise absolutely forbids. "Yours is the glory". There are two terrible examples in the Bible of men who took glory to themselves to the point where they began to think they were gods. One was Nebuchadnezzar, who decided to build a palace that would be the biggest and the best anybody had ever seen. He built the palace and it became known as one of the Seven Wonders of the World with its hanging gardens. One day, walking around the hanging gardens and looking at this magnificent palace, he said these words: "Is this not great Babylon which I have built by my mighty power as a royal residence and for the glory of my majesty?" Not a very humble man, obviously. The next few verses in the Bible say that a few days later he lost his reason and became insane. He went and lived in the woods like an animal, his nails grew long like claws and his hair grew long like feathers, and he ate grass and he was mad for a year, then he came to his senses again, and he realised what went wrong and why he had gone mad. He realised that you give God the glory, and from then on he did. God restored him and allowed him to go back to the hanging gardens of Babylon. For the rest of his life he gave glory to God for his achievements. It is a wonderful story because it finished up happily.

There is a man in the New Testament where it didn't end happily. A man called Herod (not the Herod who was alive when Jesus was born but the Herod before whom Paul appeared). This Herod one day appeared on the balcony of his palace and the crowds came. He spoke to them with great oratory. The crowds began to shout and chant: "It is the voice of a god not a man." He heard this and he accepted it, and he stood there and thought "I'm a god." The Bible says: "Because he did not give the glory to God he was eaten by worms." That man collapsed on that balcony that day and he came to the most ignominious and undignified end that a person could come to, because he did not give God the glory.

A Reith lecturer some decades ago began his lectures by saying that the technological achievements of modern man meant that man had now reached his divinity – that man had become god. When he hears that, God's jealousy overruns – the glory is God's. If there is anything that you have done that is of any value at all, give God the glory. If there is anything you have achieved, anything you have done for your fellow men and women, give God the glory.

In a church where I ministered we had a building fund to which people contributed. But I said to the congregation: read 1 Chronicles 29, because David said when he got a great result for his building fund: "O God, this was all your doing not ours. We just gave you what was yours. We couldn't have given it to you unless you gave it to us." It was then that David said: "Yours is the kingdom. Yours is the power. Yours is the glory." So whatever we do, let us give God the glory.

Do you know that becoming a Christian does this? I have spoken with many people who desperately tried to be a Christian. They tried hard to be good enough. They imitated Christians. They went to church, read the Bible, and they didn't get any nearer. Why not? Because they were trying to do it themselves. They were trying to *achieve* Christianity and you never can. Why? Because God will not let you glory in your own works lest anyone should boast. God will make you a Christian if you trust him instead of trying. We begin our Christian life utterly dependent on God. We cannot boast that we are Christians. If somebody says to me "Are you a Christian?" I will say yes, but that doesn't mean I think I am anything better than they are. It simply means that God did something for me that I could not do for myself. All the way through our Christian life, if we manage anything at all – whether in preaching, Sunday school teaching, missionary work, or in simple godly living – it is not our work, it is God's work.

It is all God's glory. The earth shall be filled with the knowledge of the glory of God as the waters cover the sea. The Bible finishes in that blaze of glory for God. But there are just two more little terms: *forever and ever* is one of them. Do you realise that there is no other kingdom, no other power, and no other glory about which you can say "For ever and ever"? There is only one kingdom that will last for ever. All the other kingdoms of the world rise and fall. I am told that there isn't a power that man has discovered that will not run out some day. Even the sun will run out of energy. Our oil and coal reserves will run out, every other power runs out, uranium will run out, but God's power is for ever.

In a bookshop I noticed a series of paperbacks: The Glory that was Rome, The Glory that was Greece – a whole series but it was all the glory that had been. The Lord's throne shall never pass away.

The last word of the Lord's Prayer is a tremendous word: *Amen*. It is not a kind of religious "Hear, hear". It is not just a convenient way of saying when you have got to the end of your prayer. "Amen" is one of the strongest words in the Hebrew language. It means "certainly, surely, inevitably, definitely, absolutely". It means: so be it. It means that you are absolutely sure that God's kingdom will never collapse, that his power will never be overcome or exhausted, and that his glory will never grow dim.